FRED KEENOR

The Man Who Never Gave Up

FRED KEENOR
The Man Who Never Gave Up

James Leighton

First published in Great Britain in 2010 by The Derby Books Publishing
Company Limited, 3 Parker Centre, Mansfield Road, Derby, DE21 4SZ.

ISBN 978-1-85983-828-0
Printed and bound by OZGraf, Poland.

CONTENTS

Acknowledgements   7

Introduction   9

Chapter 1   The Early Years   11

Chapter 2   Signing for Cardiff City AFC   23

Chapter 3   The War Years   27

Chapter 4   Getting Back to Normality   50

Chapter 5   The Start of the Glory Years   74

Chapter 6   A Season to Remember   98

Chapter 7   The Bitter Decline   125

Chapter 8   The Post-Cardiff City Years   150

Chapter 9   Fred's Legacy   159

DEDICATION

For my Dad.

ACKNOWLEDGEMENTS

This book would not have been possible without my Dad. It was his love of Cardiff City that inspired me to follow the fortunes of the Bluebirds and his encyclopedic knowledge of the game that introduced me to heroes from yesteryear such as Steve Bloomer, Dixie Dean and, of course, Fred Keenor himself. His support, encouragement and love over the years have been unparalleled!

The rest of my family has also all helped immeasurably in all kinds of different ways. I couldn't have done it without my Mum, my brother Alex, my Auntie Anita and Uncle Roy, my cousin Neil and my godfather Barry. Special mention must also go to my beloved Nan, sadly no longer with us, who always encouraged me to write.

A big thank you must also go to the official historian of Cardiff City, Richard Shepherd. Not only did he provide great enthusiasm for this project but he also contributed, from his private memorabilia collection, the many fantastic pictures of Fred Keenor that you see in this book.

Thanks must also go to Andrew Lewis who, as grandson of former Cardiff City chairman Walter Parker, has in his possession every Cardiff City programme from 1915 through to 1932. Andrew kindly let me sit in his house for hours on end as I waded through each programme.

I'm sure I must also have worn out the patience of Fred Keenor's son-in-law, Brian Jones, who made time to answer my many questions and provide me with a unique insight into Fred Keenor on and off the football pitch. His input and support for this project was invaluable.

Finally, special thanks must go to all of the team at DB Publishing for believing in this project and publishing it.

'Fred Keenor never gave up. He was one of the biggest-hearted players of all time.'
Ernie Curtis

'Fred Keenor sums up the attitude of our team. I honestly do not believe the word "beaten" is in his vocabulary.'
Fred Stewart

INTRODUCTION

In 2008 Cardiff City shocked the football world when, for the first time since 1927, they improbably reached the FA Cup Final. In contrast to their current standing in the game, Cardiff City were one of the finest sides in the country during the 1920s. It was therefore no great surprise when they famously beat Arsenal 1–0 in the 1927 Cup Final, and in the process became the first and only side from outside England to win the FA Cup.

During the build-up to the 2008 Cup Final there was plenty of media coverage of the 1927 team. We heard all about the team's lucky black cat, Trixie, the controversial goal that had won the Cup for Cardiff and how the goalscorer, Hughie Ferguson, tragically committed suicide just a few years after becoming a Cup-winner.

We also learnt that the captain, and talisman, of that 1927 Cup-winning team was Welsh international Fred Keenor. Hailed by many as the greatest player ever to have played in the blue shirt of Cardiff City, it seemed that, other than the fact that he had won the Cup, little else was known about the club's favourite son.

As an avid football and Cardiff City fan, I decided to delve deeper into Fred's background to find out more about this mysterious legend, who despite taking part in one of the greatest days in Welsh sport, had never had a book written about him or had a tribute erected in his honour.

My research led me to read every single Cardiff City programme from Fred's time at the club, as well as spending hours in the library pouring over old newspapers and football journals. Both provided me with a glimpse, not only into Fred's life, but also into a world which was in some respects far removed from the one we currently live in, but also not so very different. In addition I was fortunate to speak to officials at Cardiff City Football Club, and members of Fred's family, who all provided me with valuable nuggets of information.

Once I had completed my research I was staggered to find that there was so much more to Fred's story than the fact that he was an FA Cup-winner and Welsh captain. Not only had he enjoyed a club and international career that was littered with honours, but he had also been wounded while fighting in the trenches during World War One. Many felt that he would never be able to play football again. It was of no great surprise to learn that his typical fighting spirit not only saw him return to the game that he loved, but also helped him become one of the finest defenders of his generation.

Though Fred earned many accolades for his style of play, he also acquired a reputation as one of the game's hard men. His never-say-die attitude and rocket-propelled challenges earned him as many admirers as detractors. The over-zealous nature of some of his tackles meant that on one occasion he inspired a pitch invasion, which led to him being attacked by fans; however, Fred was never more at home than as an underdog, with a hostile crowd spitting venom in his direction, as he proved on countless occasions.

Fred's career also ran parallel to the explosion of interest in football in South Wales and the advent of its first professional team, Cardiff City. As Fred's fortunes grew, so did the fortunes of Cardiff and Wales, and as Fred suffered a downturn in luck, following his retirement, so did the club and country that he represented with such pride and determination.

Fred Keenor's life story is a rich one, full of triumphs, failures, laughter and tears. I hope that this book does justice to the man who never gave up and as a result provided Cardiff City and the Welsh national team with some of their finest moments.

CHAPTER I

THE EARLY YEARS

A Legend is Born

On 31 July 1894, the day that Fred Keenor was born, a Cardiff-based newspaper wrote an article, regarding an annual meeting of Welsh Congregationalists, which could have been written about Fred himself. The article said:

> The majority of the delegates present are men who have risen from the lowest ranks of society by the source of their own talents, and they are conscious of their strength. Very few of them show any evidence of culture but there is about them a sturdiness of character and a resoluteness of will which convinced the onlooker that they would make their mark on the future of Welsh life.

Although Fred did not quite grow up among 'the lowest ranks of society', his childhood was spent in the working-class district of Roath, Cardiff, where he shared a tiny terraced house in Theodora Street with his mother, Mary, his father, Robert, and his 10 brothers and sisters.

Robert Keenor was a highly-regarded stonemason who worked long hours in order to ensure that his 11 children did not go without. Although luxuries were few and far between in the Keenor household, his efforts meant that he was able to employ a servant so that Mary Keenor would have help looking after the children. The servant, Elizabeth Maler, was not paid well, and the bulk of her remuneration consisted of being allowed to live in the house and to receive free meals.

Conditions were not only cramped in the house, with Fred having to share a bed with three of his brothers, but they were also very basic. For instance, the house did not have an inside toilet, it only had an outhouse in the garden, which not only meant night-time sprints in the rain in order to reach it, but also meant that it had to be emptied when full. Baths could only be had once a week, due to the cost of hot water, and central heating was virtually unheard of at the turn of the century, so the winter months could be particularly harsh. Indeed, the Keenors counted themselves lucky that they even had electricity in their home, something which had only come to Cardiff in 1885.

Life was a lot harder then than it is today, with devices we take for granted either not yet invented or too expensive to purchase, such as the telephone, television and radio. Even the motor car was a toy preserved for the seriously wealthy and was an item which would cause a real stir if seen being driven down the streets of Cardiff. Most people still travelled by horse-drawn vehicles in the town until 1905, when electric trams were first introduced.

The significant number of horses still in use for travel purposes and the poor sanitation meant that the stench of manure and of the open sewers in the town must have been overwhelming. A local paper described the unseemly conditions in Stanley Street, an area not too far away from Fred's home in Roath, emphasising just how grim life was for some of the working class:

> The stench from the lower portion of the open gutter is in summer often abominable. The street, or rather pitched footway, forms the drying ground of the occupants of the houses. A clothes line, common to all, extends from one end of the alley to another and this is in fine weather constantly in use.
>
> In the summer the street forms a kind of general washhouse and women, in semi-state of nudity, whose clothes are often nothing but a

collection of dirty rags, with old earthenware pans placed on broken chairs, occupy the day.

There are about 40 houses in the street, many consisting of two rooms one over the other without a back door or an opening in the wall to give ventilation. There is scarcely a house with a window but in which a number of panes of glass are not broken and the aperture filled with old rags. There is not a house but in which the lower half of the outer door is not honey-combed and large portions eaten away by rats who in the early morning make the street and houses a kind of happy hunting ground for their species.

The bedroom is reached by a staircase rising from the lower rooms and entering the upper through an opening in the floor like a rat trap. Police found a woman and her baby sharing a wooden projection to a house which sheltered a donkey, and homeless children were often found sleeping under carts.

The conditions must have been dreadful but most did not know any better. Thankfully, the black gold of coal would soon see Cardiff become the biggest coal-exporting port in the world and would bring with it increased prosperity and improved living conditions. As a result of this Cardiff was christened 'the Chicago of Britain'.

The many opportunities that coal provided saw people flock from all over the globe to work in Cardiff, and consequently it became a boom town and one of Great Britain's largest multicultural societies. This influx of people resulted in an unprecedented surge in the population, which grew from just 20,000 inhabitants in 1851, to over 160,000 by 1901.

The majority of Cardiff's immigrants settled in the Tiger Bay district, which became a melting pot of all the world's nationalities. Tiger Bay was also a favoured destination for sailors, due to it providing many dens of iniquity, where prostitutes, alcohol and gambling were usually the order of the day. It did not take long for the area to become renowned as one of the country's most notorious districts, where many murders and crimes went unsolved and the police did not dare patrol the streets alone.

In 1905, with Cardiff gaining prominence as a result of its booming docks and increasing population, King Edward VII awarded the town city status. In order to celebrate such a momentous honour many of Cardiff's finest buildings were erected, such as the City Hall, the Law Courts, Glamorgan County Hall and the Coal and Shipping Exchange.

In order to satisfy the ever-expanding population, the leisure and entertainment options also began to grow. Subsequently many of Cardiff's best-known attractions were designed and opened during this era. One of the city's most famous parks, Roath Park, opened in 1894 and boasted a scenic lake and award-winning gardens. During Edwardian times it is estimated that as many as 2,000 people would swim in the park's lake on Sunday mornings.

Another illustrious Cardiff park, Victoria Park, was opened in 1897 in order to celebrate Queen Victoria's Diamond Jubilee. Remarkably, a seal lived in the park's lake from 1912 until its death in 1939. The seal had been found in a consignment of fish at Cardiff Docks and had been taken to the park to live. Disregarding the fact that the seal was female, she was christened 'Billy', and visitors flocked to see her. Billy's skeleton is still on show to this day at the National Museum of Wales and there is even a statue commemorating her at the park.

With Cardiff becoming a recognised destination, many of the world's famous showpeople began to visit, such as Buffalo Bill, the legendary American scout, horseman, buffalo hunter, pony express rider and showman.

Buffalo Bill and his Wild West Show had first visited Cardiff in 1891 to huge acclaim. On his return to Cardiff in 1903, a record crowd of 22,000 people packed into Sophia Gardens to watch his show, which included over 100 horses and Red Indians from the Sioux, Arapaho, Brule and Cheyenne tribes. Buffalo Bill was very fond of Wales, and during a dinner held in his honour by the Mayor of Cardiff, he told guests: 'The scenery in Wales would be hard to excel. The mountains, hills and streams remind me of my own native land. It is grand, it is beautiful and we are leaving with a great deal of regret.'

The cultural offerings in Cardiff also increased as many of the world's finest plays were put on in the city following the opening of its first theatre, the New Theatre, in 1906. The world's most critically acclaimed books were also made available to the inhabitants of Cardiff, free of charge, when Cardiff Central Library opened in 1896. These were additions gratefully received by the locals, as without the mediums of the cinema, television and radio they provided them with much sought after entertainment options.

In addition, events of a worldwide interest also occurred in the city during Fred's childhood, such as Captain Scott and his ship, the *Terra Nova*, setting sail from Cardiff at the start of his last expedition to Antarctica. Tragically, the expedition ended in disaster when Scott and his crew lost their lives on their return from the South Pole. A lighthouse has since been erected in Roath Park to pay tribute to the ultimately unsuccessful expedition.

New shopping facilities also began to spring up at a rapid rate as Cardiff became something of a shopping mecca. In 1790 there had been just 25 retail shops in Cardiff, but within 100 years this had significantly changed. Cardiff's first department store, David Morgan, opened in 1879 and this was then followed by the creation of many of Cardiff's famous shopping arcades, with the opening of the Morgan Arcade in 1879, High Street Arcade in 1885, the Castle Arcade in 1887 and Duke Street Arcade in 1902. Cardiff Central Market also opened in 1891 which provided a number of diverse stores that sold goods from all over the world.

Cardiff may have offered Fred Keenor many cultural and entertainment options, but the only thing that interested him was spending hours in the streets playing football with his friends. Footballs were expensive, however, and anyone who was lucky enough to own one would suddenly find themselves with several new best friends. If no football was available then a tennis ball would be used, but if times were really desperate then as a last resort the boys would make their own ball by tying old rags together into a tight bundle. The world of theatres, shopping and reading was certainly not one that could tempt a young Fred away from the streets, where he happily played with his friends.

If Fred had wished to pursue activities other than football, his family's low income would have no doubt prevented him from doing so in any event. Nothing would ever be given to Fred on a plate, in his own household or in life. His humble beginnings meant that he was provided with 'a sturdiness of character and a resoluteness of will' which became his enduring character trait during his football career. As will be seen, no matter the circumstances in which Fred found himself, his strength of character allowed him to prevail in most cases.

Perhaps living with 10 brothers and sisters also resulted in Fred acquiring his infamous leadership skills, as in order to have his own way he would have had to work out how best to inspire, encourage and cajole the other Keenor siblings. It is obvious that from a young age this was something that Fred was very accomplished at, not only in his own house, but also at school, as he was selected to be the captain of his primary school football team, such was the respect he had earned from his peers.

It would, of course, be the game of football that would be the 'source' of Fred's talents, and this would see him make his 'mark on the future of Welsh life'.

Fred, Cardiff and football collide

When Fred was growing up professional football was still very much in its infancy. The sport itself had only been in existence, as an organised game, in Great Britain since the beginning of the 19th century, when English public schools, such as Eton, began to play.

It took until 1863 for the laws of the game to be formalised when the Football Association was established, but it was not until 1885, just nine years before Fred's birth, that professionalism was finally legalised.

Before 1885 many clubs had been making illegal payments to players in order to boost the competitiveness of their teams. This had aroused the contempt of those clubs who were abiding by the strictly amateur laws of the Football Association, and it was therefore decided that it would be fairer if all payments to players were transparent so that there would be a relatively level playing field.

Though some teams turned professional, they would have to wait until 1888 for the Football League to be established by Aston Villa director William McGregor. The 12 clubs that played in that inaugural Football League season were Accrington Stanley, Aston Villa, Blackburn Rovers, Bolton Wanderers, Burnley, Derby County, Everton, Notts County, Preston North End, Stoke, West Bromwich Albion and Wolverhampton Wanderers. Note that all of these clubs were situated in either the Midlands or the north of England. This was partly due to the fact that travel options were limited and it would have cost a great deal of money for clubs in the north to travel via train to those clubs situated in the south.

In the year that Fred was born, 1894, the Southern League was formed and this proved vital to the development of professional football in the south of England, and eventually Wales. Initial members of the League included teams such as Reading, Millwall Athletic and Luton Town.

At this stage the closest professional side for the public of South Wales to watch on a regular basis was Bristol City. Such was the clamour to watch professional football in the region that the Great Western Railway reported that on match days more than 1,000 people would leave Cardiff to travel to Bristol in order to watch the team play.

The only team that the public of South Wales could watch play in Cardiff that included professional players would have been the Welsh national football team; however, even the opportunity to watch the Welsh team play in the city was limited, as they played their matches throughout Wales rather than in just one location. The Welsh team was nevertheless always guaranteed a large crowd when they did play in Cardiff, especially as the team boasted one of the most famous names in the game, Billy Meredith, who at the time was described as 'the finest right-winger living'.

It is estimated that Meredith played in as many as 2,000 games in a career that spanned over 30 years and would see him still playing professionally at the age of 50. Meredith is one of the elite group of players who have played for both Manchester United and Manchester City, and he is revered equally by both sets of fans, not only for his prodigious talent, but also for winning silverware at both clubs.

Another famous character playing for the Welsh team at this time was goalkeeper Leigh Richmond Roose, also known as 'the Joking Prince'. Roose was regarded as the best goalkeeper of his era, with the press saying of him: 'Everything he did was magical; he was a law unto himself'.

He certainly was a law unto himself, as one of his clubs found to their considerable cost. One day Roose missed the train that was scheduled to take him from London to Birmingham, where he was meant to be playing a match. Fearing that he might miss the game, Roose hired a VIP train just for himself and travelled back to Birmingham in luxury, leaving his club to pick up the then enormous bill of £31.

At the turn of the last century, the appetite for football in South Wales was becoming insatiable, and since there was not being a professional side to watch locally, any amateur game would attract thousands of spectators, who would crowd around the perimeter of the pitch. For instance, in 1900, one primary school match, between Albany Road School and Lansdowne Road School, saw over 600 people watch the game. It was unsurprising that games of this nature attracted such large audiences. With no television or radio available, any live sport was always rapturously received.

People did not just want to watch football, however; they were desperate to play the game as well. As a result the number of football clubs affiliated to the South Wales FA grew from just 76 in 1906 to 262 by 1910.

With the increasing popularity of football in Cardiff it was surprising that it took until 1909 for the introduction of a professional team in the city, which arrived thanks to a Bristol-born, disabled, lithographic artist called Bartley Wilson. Wilson was a keen football enthusiast who had been running the football section of the Riverside Cricket Club since 1899. He was convinced that a professional football team would prosper in Cardiff, having seen the fanatical interest there was in the sport in the city and how successful Bristol City and Bristol Rovers had been just across the River Severn.

In order to test the Cardiff public's appetite for a professional team, Wilson firstly formed an amateur side called Cardiff City AFC and set about organising a number of friendly matches against professional teams, including Crystal Palace, Bristol City and Middlesbrough.

The Middlesbrough friendly was a real coup for the fledgling club as its team boasted football superstars of the era, such as the first £1,000 player, Alf Common, as well as England international Steve Bloomer. Bloomer in particular was well known to the Welsh public, having scored five goals for England in a 9–1 win against Wales at Cardiff Arms Park in 1896.

Cardiff were definitely underdogs against Middlesbrough, yet they thrilled a crowd of thousands who turned up to watch the game at the Harlequins Athletic Ground when they emerged as unlikely 2–1 winners. Subsequent high attendances and gate receipts in the other friendly games were encouraging enough to persuade Wilson that he had been correct in thinking that a professional team in Cardiff would be a success.

It appears that the organisers of the Southern League agreed with Wilson, as within weeks of Cardiff's victory over Middlesbrough the club was invited to join the Second Division of the Southern League. This was a major result for Bartley Wilson, as his dream had been realised of providing a professional football team to the city of Cardiff.

At this stage the next step was for the club to find itself a permanent home that met with Southern League standards. Surprisingly, the club found that home on a rubbish tip adjacent to the railway sidings, in an area of Cardiff called Leckwith. Cardiff City received invaluable help in getting the ground up to the required standard from Lord Ninian Crichton-Stuart, who helped bankroll the development. The home of Cardiff City was subsequently named Ninian Park in his honour.

A supporter who helped with the development at Ninian Park described just how the stadium was constructed:

It had been decided that the area which sloped away from the railway should be built up to form an embankment along the length of the playing pitch, the site of which had been stalked out and ran parallel to Sloper Road.

We proceeded to dig and level the site of the pitch, wheeling the spoil in barrows to the far side where it was tipped to form the bank. The contractors arranged with the Corporation for refuse to be tipped onto the bank, while the local factories and the gasworks on Penarth Road sent along ashes and clinker from their furnaces, until enough material had been tipped to form quite a substantial bank.

The spectators who later came to stand on this bank suffered whenever there was a stiff wind, since the dust and ashes flew up causing them to resemble coal-miners who had worked a hard day at the pit. To complete the embankment, large wooden hoardings were built along the top to prevent free viewing and access to the railway.

As the ground was built on a former rubbish tip, items such as glass and stones would regularly work their way to the surface of the pitch. On mornings prior to a game, players, officials and supporters would scour the pitch for items that could cause any harm. These pre-match searches were not always a success, as the club's first-ever professional player, Jack Evans, found to his cost when he sliced his knee on a piece of glass protruding through the pitch and was left scarred for life. Evans, also known as 'the Bala Bang', contributed to the formation of Ninian Park when he helped build a wooden grandstand in the stadium, for which he was paid 35 shillings a week.

The advent of professionalism also saw Cardiff reconsider their chocolate and amber quarter kit and instead wear blue shirts for the very first time. These blue shirts subsequently led to Cardiff City earning its nickname, the Bluebirds. In 1911 a play was being shown at Cardiff's New Theatre called *The Blue Bird*. The play gained a substantial amount of publicity and shortly afterwards it is thought that fans of Cardiff City christened their team the Bluebirds in homage to the popular play and the team's blue shirts.

After all of Bartley Wilson's hard work he must have been delighted to see Cardiff play their first-ever game at Ninian Park on I September 1910, when the Bluebirds played host to Aston Villa in a friendly. Cardiff lost the game 2–1, with Jack Evans creating history by becoming the first player to score a goal at the ground, but the 7,000 spectators that were at the game loved every minute of it. The *Western Mail* was equally as rapturous as the fans when giving its verdict on the game:

> The Cardiff City Association Football Club has every reason to congratulate itself on the success of the inaugural match with Aston Villa yesterday. Not only did the players give an excellent account of themselves, but they managed to raise the enthusiasm of some 7,000 spectators. Besides Lord Ninian Stuart and Mr D.A. Thomas, MP, there were many prominent people among the spectators, as well as a number of Welsh rugby players, who evinced much interest in the game.

Not everyone in South Wales heralded the arrival of a professional football team in the area, however. Rugby had always been the predominant sport in the region, but the arrival of football had seen thousands of fans desert the supposed 'national game'. This led to an intense rivalry between the two sports in South Wales, with rugby being classed as the traditional sport, led by the blazer brigade, and football being seen as the brash, new, working-class game. Many in the rugby community were also dismissive of football as a professional sport, as the rugby code steadfastly remained true to its amateur roots.

Football's success was so rapid that many rugby fans began to fret that it was overtaking the popularity of their own sport. Consequently, the Welsh Rugby Union was berated for not doing more to counter football's efforts. The *Western Mail* wrote that the Welsh Rugby Union was showing: 'with characteristic apathy, a masterly inactivity which makes one despair'.

The newspaper also wrote about football's new-found popularity after watching the thousands of spectators attend an early Cardiff City game:

> The game had all the intensity of a Cup tie, being fast and furious – sometimes literally furious – from beginning to end, and as an example

of the concentrated excitement that can be conveyed by Association football, must have gone far to complete the conversion of the many one-time Rugby enthusiasts who witnessed the sport.

To argue any longer that 'Soccer' is not a serious menace to 'Rugger' in the Welsh metropolis is tantamount to betraying an ignorance of existing facts and a narrow, prejudiced outlook of possible future developments. It was only a qualifying round between two second-rate teams in the English Cup competition and yet the match magnetized an assemblage of nearly 13,000 souls.

The arrival of professional football in Cardiff could not have come at a better time for Fred Keenor. He had just finished school and was eager to play football for a living. The newly-formed professional team gave him a realistic opportunity to achieve his dream.

Although Fred started playing football at a young age, it was at Stacey Road Primary School that his football ability, and leadership skills, first began to flourish. It was here that Fred played organised football for the first time, rather than just in the street with his friends. As previously mentioned, his leadership skills were obviously evident at a young age as he was selected to captain the school football team. The team he captained was a talented one, as it once went a whole season without losing a match and subsequently won the local school championship.

Fred's natural talent for football meant that he was soon called upon to represent Cardiff's schoolboy team. His stellar performances for the Cardiff schoolboy team caught the eye of the Welsh youth-team selectors and as a result, in 1907, he was selected to play in the very first Schoolboy international against England. In his professional days Fred would make his reputation as a hardened defender, but he was surprisingly selected to play as an outside-right for Wales.

Fred's reputation as a promising young footballer would soon see him get noticed by the newly-formed professional team in Cardiff, and what would follow would be an unprecedented period of success for the team and for Fred Keenor.

CHAPTER 2

SIGNING FOR CARDIFF CITY AFC

The Big Break

In 1912, Fred's dream of playing professional football took a huge leap forward when he was invited to take part in a trial game for Cardiff City. It was coincidentally an old schoolmaster of Fred's, Walter Riden, who was by now a director at Cardiff City, who had invited Fred to the trial. Riden had witnessed Fred playing for amateur side Roath Wednesday, and had admired his wholehearted display. Fred would later describe this as being 'one of the big moments in my life, I did not think twice about it'.

During his trial at the club Fred impressed and as a result he was offered an amateur contract. Not long after signing for Cardiff he played several games for the amateur side in the Western League, as one of the 'great unpaid'.

The Western League comprised teams such as Bristol Rovers Reserves, Bath City, Peasedown, Paulton, Camerton, Weymouth and Welton Rovers. With the exception of Bristol Rovers and Bath City, the teams were not very strong and Cardiff usually won the games at a canter; however, Fred recalled that in the lead up to a match against Camerton the team were too relaxed and had arrogantly predicted that they would walk the game. This attitude cost them dearly as they lost 3–1. Fred would carry the lesson with him for the rest of his career. He later said: 'In subsequent seasons I always thought of that game when we were supposed to be on a "good thing". It has a moral which I pass on to every young footballer.'

Notwithstanding the defeat to Camerton, Fred's impressive performances for the amateur side were being noted at the club. In 1912, a Cardiff City programme commented on Fred's potential: 'Keenor is another player who has shown great promise and I believe he will go far'.

It was, in fact, hard to ignore Fred. He had arrived at Cardiff City like a tornado, not content to sit quietly in the background and determined to get himself noticed. He was not the tallest, biggest or most talented player at the club, but that did not stop him barracking senior players if he felt they were not playing to their potential. He was not all talk either; he ran tirelessly for the cause and would frequently put his body on the line in order to quell opposition attacks. His endeavours could only inspire his teammates to reach a higher standard of play.

At this time Fred was not the captain of the amateurs, let alone the reserves, but he was like a general on the pitch, dictating the play and urging his teammates to run into certain positions. Although he was of small stature, his attitude and charisma made him appear like a giant. Many a time throughout his career he would intimidate players much larger than himself with his aggression and gargantuan efforts.

As a result of his encouraging displays for the amateur side the club offered Fred a professional contract that would pay him the princely sum of 10 shillings a week. In addition to this, Fred also continued to work as a labourer and therefore earned two salaries, which he said made him 'feel like a millionaire'. This was a status that the city of Cardiff would also become renowned for, when, in 1913, the first-ever £1 million business deal was said to have been struck in the Coal Exchange.

It was fortunate for Fred that his arrival in the professional game coincided with the arrival of Cardiff City's most successful-ever manager, Fred Stewart. In 1911 the club had advertised the vacant position of secretary-manager in a publication called *Athletic News*, which was a magazine widely read by football fans throughout the UK.

The advert had resulted in the appointment of Fred Stewart as the club's first-ever full-time secretary-manager when he took over from player-manager Davy McDougall. Stewart was highly experienced in such a role, with 18 years of experience as secretary-manager of Stockport County behind him. His contract was initially only scheduled to last for a three-year period, but Stewart stayed with Cardiff City until 1933, winning numerous honours along the way.

In order for Stewart to carry out his duties as manager, George Latham, who had been signed for Cardiff City from Stoke the previous season, assisted him as the team's trainer. The partnership of Stewart as manager, Latham as trainer and, eventually, Fred as captain, would in time bring many memorable times to the fans of Cardiff City.

As soon as Stewart arrived at the club he set about improving the small, youthful squad. His first signings included experienced professional players such as Arthur Waters, Bob Leah, Harry Featherstone, Harry Tracey, Eddie Thompson and Jack Burton.

One of the most significant signings Stewart made as manager of Cardiff City at this time was that of left-half Billy Hardy from Stockport County. Stewart had actually bought Hardy when he was manager of Stockport, and he was so desperate to be reacquainted with him that he paid the £25 transfer fee himself. His judgement proved to be shrewd, as Hardy stayed at Cardiff City until 1932 and blossomed into one of the best left half-backs in the Football League.

Though Stewart signed a number of players, he had also noted Fred's talent and was eager to introduce him into the first team; however, Fred's chances were limited due to Cardiff having one of the strongest defences in the League and the fact that at that time a team was also not allowed to name substitutes. Fred would have to bide his time and wait for someone to suffer an injury or loss of form before he could get his chance.

Towards the end of the 1912–13 season, in which Cardiff City won the Second Division of the Southern League, Fred finally got an opportunity to impress Stewart in two first-team friendly games. He made his first-team debut against Bridgend YMCA, where he scored one of the goals in a 9–0 win, and he then played in a 1–1 draw against Mid Rhondda.

In spite of delivering impressive displays in the friendly games, Fred was frustrated to find that as the 1913–14 season kicked-off he would continue to ply his trade in the reserve team. This did not deter him, however, as he continued to put in scintillating performances and many were now alerted to the fact that Cardiff might have a young jewel in their squad. After one reserve game a match report said of Fred's performance: 'Davidson, McKenzie and Keenor did their share of the defence and did it very well. The latter gives promise of great things and will prove a valuable substitute should one of the "holy three" get injured in the first team.'

The 'holy three' referred to were Cardiff's half-back line of 'Kidder' Harvey, Cassidy and Hardy, who were recognised as the best defensive unit in the Southern League. In spite of their formidable reputation, Fred's performances in the reserves had started to put pressure on the 'holy three' as he continued to earn promising reviews: 'Another man who did himself the fullest justice was Keenor. We predict a brilliant future for this player if he goes on as he has started.'

On 6 December 1913, Fred finally made his Southern League debut for Cardiff City when he took part in the 1–1 home draw with Exeter City. He was, however, no doubt feeling the weight of expectation on his young shoulders as he put in a nervous display, with local reports saying that he was 'the weak link in a very strong side'.

It was of no surprise that Fred did not feature in the first team again until 27 December, when he played in Cardiff's 2–1 win over Plymouth Argyle. After these two performances it appears that Stewart felt that Fred was not quite ready to become a first-team regular as he made only one more first-team appearance that season when he played in a 0–0 draw against Millwall.

With a handful of first-team appearances now behind him, and further encouraging displays for the reserves, Fred would have no doubt felt that the 1914–15 season could finally be the year when he would get a prolonged run in the side, however, Fred's fledgling career was stopped in its tracks by the outbreak of World War One. Life would never be the same for Fred, or his teammates, as they went off to fight for their country. Some of them would never return.

CHAPTER 3

THE WAR YEARS

Season 1914–15

By the time that Cardiff City had lost their opening fixture at Watford virtually all of Europe was at war. Even though World War One was still in its infancy more than 2,000 British soldiers had already lost their lives.

The outbreak of the war came at a terrible time for Fred's football career. Though he had not featured in the loss to Watford, he did play in the next game against Norwich City, and then racked up four consecutive first-team appearances for which he gained much praise.

For instance, the *Athletic News*, while being critical of the Cardiff City team's performance against Brighton and Hove Albion, had nothing but admiration for Fred:

> Keenor, who occupied the pivot position owing to an injury sustained by Cassidy in the Gillingham match, has just turned 20 and is a product of Cardiff school football.
>
> One can safely predict a brilliant future for him, providing, of course, he is well looked after. On Saturday he was a menace both to the Brighton attack and defence. One minute he would be tackling a Brighton forward, the next he would be leading Cardiff forwards. He is a sound tackler, places perfectly, is a hard worker and can be of great

assistance to his forwards both in feeding them and taking part in combined movements.

Despite receiving many eulogies, Fred could still not dislodge any of Cardiff's renowned defenders when they returned to the side. As a result he did not play a game for the first team between 10 October 1914 and 2 January 1915.

Over the period that Fred was out of the team the war intensified, as did criticism of the football authorities for refusing to cancel the League season and not doing enough to encourage footballers to enlist.

Many in the UK had felt that the conflict would be a brief affair, and as such the FA had decided not to cancel any games. However, it did issue a statement appealing to all football supporters to do what they could to aid the war effort: 'The Football Association earnestly appeals to the patriotism of all who are interested in the game to help in all possible ways in support of the nation in the present serious crisis, and particularly to those who are able, to render personal service in the Army and Navy, which are so gallantly upholding our national honour.'

The FA's position in refusing to suspend the football season was in stark contrast to rugby's response. For example, in South Wales, Cardiff Rugby Football Club had cancelled its fixtures for the forthcoming season as early as 1 September 1914. Moreover, 11 of the Senghenydd rugby team, which had been virtually wiped out in a mining disaster just a year before, had enlisted as soon as the war had broken out.

With the rugby community eagerly assisting the war effort, some in South Wales questioned whether the football community was doing enough. There had always been an uneasy relationship between the supporters of the perceived national sport of rugby and the supporters of the new, working-class sport of football. Many football fans felt that rugby supporters were blowing the situation out of all proportion in order to take the rare opportunity to criticise their sport, and this meant that the disagreements between the two intensified.

The local press in South Wales were particularly scathing about the efforts of Cardiff City, due to the club refusing to cancel fixtures and the players and fans being reluctant to enlist. Subsequently a frenzy of criticism was unleashed. Below is just a selection of the comments that were printed in the *Western Mail* newspaper regarding Cardiff City's war efforts:

- 'On Saturday I felt quite sick that so many able-bodied young men could lose themselves in an exciting match. After discounting the soldiers, old people, ladies and children present, it seemed to me that there were quite 5,000 young fellows present who would be gladly accepted by the recruiting officers. The 22 players were fine specimens of manhood. How much nobler it would have been if they had rifles on their shoulders marching to the battlefield, instead of playing with a leather-encased bladder.'

- 'I consider that professional football has eternally disgraced itself by forsaking the country at the present critical time. It has committed a crime for which it will never be pardoned, and which will be cast into its face for untold years to come.'

- 'Soccer matches still attract thousands of spectators, out of whom there must be a large crowd of young fellows – "cowards" we call them – who, instead of watching football matches should be training to fight for their King and country.'

On 5 September 1914, Cardiff City answered the criticism directed towards its efforts when it stated in a match programme:

It will be interesting no doubt to learn that Cardiff City AFC has supplied to the forces of our country no less than seven of their signed players. This is not a bad percentage. If all clubs throughout the country did as well, it would no doubt form the nucleus of a fine body of men.

It will be gratifying for many to learn that no time has been wasted by Cardiff City directors in placing at the disposal of the local military all the resources of the club.

Fred Stewart pointed out the choice of the players were prepared to undergo a course of military training with the object of relieving the more experienced men who are at present guarding bridges etc.

He explained that far from being indifferent to their responsibilities, every man was anxious (and indeed eager) to show that they are animated by a loyal and patriotic spirit, and desirous of helping all in their power.

This response did not appease the local press, as it continued its onslaught on the club. The *Western Mail* even went so far as to refuse to report on any Cardiff City matches whatsoever. In a match programme, dated 19 September 1914, the club spelled out its discontent about its treatment by the media:

The opposition to the playing of football matches is both humorous and (in a few instances) contemptible.

Humorous because it emanates in many cases from people who are always adverse to football, and their effort to stand on a high moral pedestal and denounce football because of what they call 'the want of patriotism' on the part of players and spectators is too funny to deceive anyone.

One, however, can only have contempt for those who denounce football because they think they are in for a little cheap popularity during the present crisis.

Among these are to be found a few newspapers and we regret to note that in Cardiff we have been inflicted with considerable opposition from a quarter to which we had a right to look for more consideration. The *Western Mail* and *Evening Express* have derived considerable revenue in the past from reporting football matches and we expect they will look to the same source for revenue in the future. Yet not content with a decision to suppress the publication of football news, they have taken every opportunity to gird at players and spectators at Ninian Park.

Last week they published a photograph taken at Ninian Park and another at Cardiff Arms Park to show the comparison between events taking place at each ground in order to belittle and intimidate the club.

After the ungrudging assistance given them at all times by the management it savours of a contemptible ingratitude to treat the club in this way.

It is well known that all the Cardiff City players have offered their services for home defence, that they are subscribing a weekly sum towards the War Fund, that seven of the signed players have joined the colours, and that the War Fund will benefit to the extent of 60 pound as the result of practice matches. Yet these are the men whom the papers mentioned find it a congenial task to belittle on every occasion possible.

The *Western Mail* refused to back down and lambasted the football authorities for refusing to cancel games and the players for not voluntarily enlisting:

What would the professional clubs have to offer the country if football were to cease for a season? There are about 400 clubs, employing 7,000 players. A first League club today has anything from 18 to 35 players on its salary list. These men are trained and watched over like the gladiators they are. Physically they are the pick of the youth of the country. Lord Kitchener may be content to ask for men 5ft 3in in height, but such a standard would be laughed at by the business manager of a first League club. The average height is in the neighbourhood of 5ft 9in, and the weight well over 11st. These things have to be if victories are to be won.

The fans, players, management and directors of Cardiff City were furious by what they saw as a biased attack on football, while other sports remained unscathed. On 17 November 1914, the club again hit back at the *Western Mail*:

The local paper referred to has taken the stand that during the present War football should be stopped, and players and spectators who are eligible should join the colours; and in order to discountenance the continued playing of the game they have stopped issuing their football edition and reporting football to any extent.

On the face of it this appears to be taking a very high and patriotic stand. But is it? They have not yet stopped the supply of horse-racing reports or attempted to discourage those who support the Turf by eliminating tips from their columns.

Why not? Where is the discretion?

It seems to us that the only way to stop the opposition of this paper is to turn the ground into a race course and thus provide opportunities for the publication of tips to its readers.

The debate regarding football's attitude towards the war was not confined to South Wales. Many national newspapers and prominent figures joined in the condemnation and voiced their dissatisfaction with the football community's war efforts.

A.F. Pollard, a famous historian at the time, wrote to *The Times* newspaper to express his disgust towards professional football: 'Every club that employs a professional football player is bribing a needed recruit to refrain from enlistment, and every spectator who pays his gate money is contributing so much towards a German victory.'

Furthermore, the Poet Laureate, Robert Bridges, also joined in the debate: 'I certainly voice the feeling of the country in declaring that it is high time that professional football should be discontinued. It is high time that our footballers let the world see what they are really made of and that they do not deserve the execration that is falling upon them.'

Some leading public figures decided that in order to encourage more fans and players to enlist they would visit football matches throughout the country. Their well-intentioned efforts were ultimately unsuccessful, with just six recruits coming forward at the Cardiff City against Bristol Rovers match and none at all at Arsenal, Chelsea, Notts County, Nottingham Forest or Brighton & Hove Albion.

These poor figures were noted by *The Times* newspaper when it said of football fans' lacklustre response towards the war: 'This failure contrasts strongly with the wholesale volunteering which has distinguished the performers and devotees of other forms of sport. Rugby Union clubs, cricket elevens and rowing clubs throughout the kingdom have poured men into the ranks.'

The FA once again sought to defend its members against such fierce criticism when it wrote to *The Times* and stated: 'It is claimed by members of the Council of the Football Association that upwards of 100,000 recruits for the Army have been secured from the ranks of Association Football, and that this total exceeds by far the combined recruits who have enlisted from all other branches of sport.'

In December 1914, in order to help encourage further players and fans to enlist, William Joynson-Hicks, Unionist MP for Brentford, was charged with forming a footballers' battalion. His first objective was to entice London-based professional footballers to enlist. Subsequently, on 14 December 1914, a meeting at Fulham Town Hall was arranged with representatives of all London clubs in attendance, in order to discuss the Footballers' Battalion.

At the meeting it was proposed that the battalion would consist of 1,350 men and its ranks would be open to all those interested in the amateur or professional game. The Battalion HQ would be situated at Richmond Athletic Ground and would be known as the '17th (Service) Battalion (Football), Middlesex Regiment'.

With a specially designated footballers' battalion in place, many players and supporters now began to enlist. Perhaps one of its most successful recruits would turn out to be a 32-year-old professional footballer by the name of Frank Buckley.

Buckley had already seen previous military service when, in 1900, at the age of 18, he had enlisted in the King's Liverpool Regiment. In 1903, after buying himself out of the army, Buckley went on to play professional football for

Aston Villa, Brighton, Manchester United, Manchester City, Birmingham City, Derby County and Bradford City. He also earned a solitary England cap in a 3–0 defeat to Ireland.

While Buckley had enjoyed varied success as a player, it was as a manager after the war that he excelled, as he went on to manage clubs such as Blackpool, Wolves, Notts County, Hull City and Leeds United. His tenure at each of these clubs may not have resulted in an abundance of silverware, but it was his coaching ability, eye for a good player and acumen in the transfer market that saw him make his reputation. During his time in management he was responsible for bringing Stan Cullis and Billy Wright into the Wolves team and John Charles and Jack Charlton into the Leeds team.

Buckley was also not afraid to stand up for himself, even in the face of authority. Having once struck an opponent in the face, he was called before the FA committee to explain himself. One member of that committee recalled that Buckley 'frankly told us he had struck the man, and that he would do the same again if necessity arose. The other man he said used filthy language every time he came near an opponent, and as he persisted after being warned "he let him have it".'

In spite of the fact that Buckley would speak frankly and forcefully if required, he was also renowned for having a soft centre. Jack Charlton, the former Republic of Ireland manager and England World Cup-winner, reminisced about the first time that he met Buckley: 'Beneath the gruff exterior, he was a kind man, as he demonstrated once when I met him. My shoes must have been a sight, for when he looked down at them, he asked me if they were the only pair I had. I nodded. The next morning, he summoned me to his office and handed me a pair of Irish brogues, the strongest, most beautiful shoes I'd ever seen. And I had them for years.'

It seems that Buckley had the respect of men on the battlefield as well as on the football pitch. As Colonel Fenwick recalls: 'If I was walking down the lines with Major Buckley – no matter where we were – the men would salute in the ordinary way, but they took no further notice of me. Their eyes were for Buckley. They whispered "That's Buckley – the footballer".'

For the duration of the war, Buckley used his ability to gain respect, motivate, encourage and stand up for himself to great effect. He was promoted to the rank of Major and consequently would forever be referred to in the football world as 'the Major'.

With famous footballers such as Frank Buckley enlisting, more football players and supporters were encouraged to join the battalion. In early 1915 the battalion secured its most famous recruit when Chelsea and England international Vivian Woodward joined its ranks.

In an incredible career Woodward had scored 96 goals in 193 appearances for Spurs and 29 goals in just 23 games for England. He had also captained the Great Britain team to consecutive gold medals in the 1908 and 1912 Olympic Games. In the years immediately preceding the war, Woodward had made over 100 FA Cup and League appearances for Chelsea.

Another famous recruit to become a member of the Footballers' Battalion was Walter Tull, who was of mixed ethnicity and alleged to be the son of a slave. After impressing as an amateur for Clapton Orient, Tull signed for Tottenham Hotspur in 1909, but struggled to find his form, in part due to the continual racist abuse he suffered. After making just 12 appearances for Spurs, he signed for Northampton Town in 1911 and went on to feature in over 100 games for the Cobblers before enlisting with the Footballers' Battalion on 21 December 1914. In spite of racism being prevalent at this time, Tull was very well respected within the battalion and as a result was promoted to the rank of Lance-Sergeant. Tragically, Lance-Sergeant Tull was killed in 1918 while fighting in France.

Tull's former club, Northampton Town, erected a memorial to him in 1999 that bore the following words: 'Through his actions W.D.J. Tull ridiculed the barriers of ignorance that tried to deny people of colour equality with their contemporaries. His life stands testament to a determination to confront those people and those obstacles that sought to diminish him and the world in which he lived. It reveals a man, though rendered breathless in his prime, whose strong heart still beats loudly.'

Even though criticism of football was still rife for those continuing to play the game, there was praise for those who had enlisted. One officer in the battalion was quoted as saying:

I am particularly proud of the men who have come forward. Some of them have been very queer people to manage on the field, and I had my doubts about them submitting to military rule. But the result of the very first day in camp was astonishing. I will give you an instance, as you know_____ has an extraordinary temperament, and the day after we came here, I had occasion to ask him to render me a little personal service. He saluted me as satisfactorily as one need wish for, carried out our mission and, when I offered to thank him, he interposed with a 'No Thanks, Sir, delighted to serve you,' saluted and went on with his business.

With more footballers now enlisting, Keenor, who was a very patriotic man, was faced with a difficult dilemma. In January 1915 he had finally broken into the first team and played in 16 of the first team's next 18 games, his longest run in the team to date. He was therefore very reluctant to enlist and leave just as he had finally achieved his ambition of becoming an established first-team player. On the other hand, as a patriotic, young, fit, single man he was also expected to do his duty and join up.

His sense of duty towards his country prevailed, and despite finally breaking into the first team, Fred enlisted in the Footballers' Battalion in February 1915 along with Cardiff goalkeeper Jack Stephenson. Trainer George Latham, club directors Doctor William Nicholson and Frederick Schroeter, and the club's benefactor, Lord Ninian Crichton-Stuart, also enlisted in the armed forces at this time.

Fred's army recruitment form reveals just how small he was for a defender. The form states that Fred measured just 5ft 6¾in in height, with a chest measurement of just 37½in. Thankfully, Fred's heart and fighting spirit were a lot bigger than his physical measurements.

The news of Fred's enlistment was broken to Cardiff City fans in the next match programme:

Our readers will be interested to learn that both Keenor and Stephenson have enlisted in the Footballers' Battalion, a Middlesex Regiment. The authorities have so arranged that all footballers who enlist are allowed a free pass from London to rejoin their clubs when required, so that the contracts entered into on both sides shall not be interfered with.

They have followed the gleam which points the way to duty, and duty has no place for fear. May their example be followed by those who are able to take it, for duty inspired by patriotism is a path which all may tread.

Every weekend Fred would ensure that he would religiously catch the train from London to wherever Cardiff were playing in order to make the most of his opportunity in the first team. For the rest of the season, whenever Fred played in the team, he would be referred to on the team sheet, printed in the match programme, as 'Private Keenor'.

Shortly after enlisting, in a game against Portsmouth, Fred had to deputise in the team at centre-forward, and he duly got himself on the score sheet. In the next week's match programme Fred's performance in the forward line was lauded: 'Keenor at centre-forward made the most use of his opportunities by notching the second goal. Owing to Geo. West's injury, Keenor has again taken his place at centre-forward, a choice which will prove popular in view of his performance last Saturday'.

While Fred was soon back playing in his usual position at right-half, his versatility meant that if necessary he could cover most positions on the pitch. In a game at Reading he filled in for the injured left-half Billy Hardy, and again won plaudits for his display: 'Keenor proved a worthy substitute for Hardy. In saying that I am paying Keenor the highest compliment possible. His kicking and tackling were perfect. To accomplish the latter he seems to have copied the style of Harvey, and is demonstrating his ability to throw himself at the ball with equal ability. Soldiering seems to agree with him, as through a fast game he followed the ball with untiring persistency.'

Fred also earned rave reviews when he played at centre-half: 'Cassidy's place last week was well filled by Keenor, who has proved himself a worthy deputy to our brilliant centre-half.'

And after another scintillating performance at centre-half it was said: 'Keenor also proved a worthy substitute to Cassidy, whose place he was called upon to fill owing to the indisposition of the latter. As one who has always held the highest opinion of Keenor's ability as a player, I was glad to see my views so worthily upheld.'

In all Fred made a total of 22 first-team appearances during the season, the most he had played as a professional. The team also had a successful season as they finished in a highly respectable third place in the First Division of the Southern League.

Notwithstanding this, the season almost ended in acrimony for Cardiff City when there was 'a spot of bother' at the club regarding payments to the players. The club had been suffering financially due to poor gates, as not only had a number of supporters enlisted and left South Wales, but travel to the games in Cardiff was also restricted due to the railways being commandeered for the war effort. The *Yorkshire Post* had reported that at this time football clubs' gates were less than half the average of the three preceding seasons.

The precarious financial predicament at Cardiff City was so serious that the directors asked all of the players to take a salary cut. The players were also informed that they should seek alternative work during the summer off-season as the club might not be able to afford to pay them. This subsequent appeal was made in a match programme:

It is unthinkable that in a great industrial centre such as Cardiff, the services of such men such as Cassidy, Goddard, Layton, Kneeshaw, Hardy and many others, should be lost to the club for want of about four months' work.

It behoves us all therefore to do something towards that end. It is not someone else's business. If you care an atom for the future of the club you are asked to interest yourself earnestly in this project. Maybe you are working in a fitting shop, or some other place, where the services of a healthy, able-bodied man is required. If so, drop a line to Mr Stewart (secretary-manager), 2 Pentre Street, Grange, and he will use his judgement to choose a player best fitted for the work.

Let us all help. If we do so earnestly, the difficulty will be easily overcome. The position in which the players find themselves demands our ungrudging sympathy and help. It can best be described by Shakespeare:

> You take my house when you take the prop
> That doth sustain my house: you take my life
> When you do take the means by which I live.

As a result of this dilemma a number of players threatened to go on strike. The club directors subsequently asked Fred whether he would be prepared to raise a team from the amateurs and professionals serving with the battalion, in case the Cardiff players did go through with their threat. Thankfully for Fred this event never occurred and he did not have to choose between joining his teammates on strike or forming a Cardiff City team from the recruits of the Footballers' Battalion.

At the end of the season the FA finally bowed to pressure when it postponed the 1915–16 season and made the following statement:

> The Council, having carefully considered the present and future prospects of the game, and recognizing the paramount duty of every man to help carry on the war to a victorious issue at the earliest possible moment, and not to do anything that will in any degree postpone or hinder the desired result, resolve that for the present the following Regulations shall be observed:

- That no international matches, or the Challenge Cup and Amateur Cup matches of this Association, be played during the next season.
- That Association, Leagues and Clubs be allowed to arrange matches without cups, medals, or other awards, to suit local conditions, provided that they do not interfere with the work of those engaged in war work. Clubs may join any combination of clubs, which may be convenient to them.
- That matches be played on Saturday afternoons, and on early closing and other recognized holidays.
- That no remuneration shall be paid to players, nor shall there be any registration of players, but clubs and players shall be subject to the rules and conditions applicable to them on 30 April 1915.
- Agreements with players for service after 30 April 1915 shall be suspended until further order.

On 24 April 1915, with the football season at an end and no forthcoming season to prepare for, Fred and his fellow battalion recruits received orders to take up training at the country residence of the battalion's founder, William Joynson-Hicks, in Holmbury St Mary, near Dorking. The battalion had by now 1,400 men within its ranks.

One of the things the recruits were trained in was rifle shooting, in preparation for duty on the front line. Shooting was clearly not one of Fred's talents, however, as a Sergeant Major told him that he was the worst rifle marksman he had ever met. In an interview after the war, Fred revealed that he liked to go rabbit shooting but still suffered from a poor shot: 'I'm beginning to think that when the R.S.M. of the 17th Middlesex declared, during the war, that I was the worst shot he had ever met, he was correct.'

However, Fred's poor shooting was not limited to a rifle. Ernie Curtis, a 1927 Cardiff City teammate of Fred's, would remark that Fred had the worst shot in the Football League. Fred himself would also later admit that his shooting on the football pitch was far from perfect, when he said:

'Good shooting was never a strong point of mine. I can hear the roar of the crowd now as I remove another slate on the Canton stand.'

Although there was plenty of military training involved, the members of the battalion also occasionally found the time to organise football matches against professional teams. As could be expected, the battalion had a strong side considering it was made up of some of the best players in the country. Indeed, such was the strength of the team that a young Fred Keenor would sometimes find it hard to get a game.

One game that Fred did take part in was when the Footballers' Battalion played an exhibition game against Cardiff City at Ninian Park on 2 October 1915. Fred had been due to play for the battalion in the game, but at Fred Stewart's insistence he lined up for Cardiff City. Cardiff lost the game 1–0, but the match was described as 'a brilliant exhibition of soccer by some of the stars of the football world'.

Soon, however, Fred and the battalion would have to put all thoughts of football to one side, as they would have to brace themselves for the serious matter of fighting on the front line.

Going to the Front Line

On 16 November 1915, Fred and the Footballers' Battalion nervously started their journey to France in order to reach the front. After hours of travelling through treacherous conditions, the battalion finally arrived at billets in the small agricultural village of Les Ciseaux. Fred recalls that on reaching their destination: 'We did no actual fighting for a time, parapet guards, wiring and fatigues being the order of the day with an occasional game of football behind the lines, with the guns beating any Ninian Park roar. After a month of this we went back to Bethune for a rest, and it was here we played several matches against different regimental sides.'

Playing football no doubt stopped the players from thinking too hard about the atrocities that awaited them. However, the reality of why they were all in France finally dawned on them on 9 December 1915, when the battalion marched to Annequin, where their new billets were now only a few miles from the front line.

The following evening members of the battalion had their first taste of the war when they made their way to the trenches. Joe Bailey, a player for Reading, said that the weather was so bad that 'the mud and water was up to our waists'.

The trenches were a horror that many were not prepared for, as the comforts of life as a footballer were quickly forgotten. Millions of rats infested the trenches, gorging themselves on human remains. With so much fresh flesh on offer for the rats to feast on, many grew to be the size of cats. The soldiers, exasperated and terrified of these giant rats (which would even scamper across their faces in the dark), would attempt to rid the trenches of them by either shooting them, spearing them with bayonets or even by clubbing them to death.

No matter how often the men went on rat-killing sprees, they could never seem to get rid of the vicious vermin. This was not surprising as a single rat couple could produce up to 900 offspring in a year, spreading infection and contaminating food in their wake.

Rats were by no means the only source of infection and nuisance. Lice were a never-ending problem, breeding in the seams of filthy clothing and causing men to itch incessantly. Even when clothing was periodically washed and deloused, lice eggs invariably remained hidden in the seams and within a few hours of the clothes being reworn the body heat generated would cause the eggs to hatch. Lice also caused 'trench fever', a particularly painful disease that began suddenly with severe pain followed by a high fever, which could take 12 weeks to recover from.

Nits were another nightmare that the soldiers had to contend with. Many men were so fed up of constantly itching that they chose to shave their heads entirely to rid themselves of this scourge.

The cold, wet, and unsanitary conditions also caused another common ailment known as 'trench foot'. This was a fungal infection of the feet which in severe cases could turn a limb gangrenous, which would result in amputation of the rotten foot.

Amid all the squalid conditions there was also an offensive reek pervading the trenches, primarily owing to the rotting human carcasses lying around in their thousands in no man's land and overflowing latrines. Men who had not been afforded the luxury of a bath in weeks or months would smell of dried sweat, while athlete's foot gave off an equally abhorrent odour. Add to this the lingering stench of poisonous gas, rotting sandbags, stagnant mud and cigarette smoke, and it was a grim concoction that the soldiers had to suffer. Matters were not helped by the atrocious standard of food that the soldiers were expected to eat.

The Footballers' Battalion not only had to persevere under these trying circumstances, but they also had to become accustomed to the monotonous routine of duty in the trenches. Half an hour before dawn the men would stand on the trench fire step with their bayonets fixed in anticipation of a German attack, and would not stand down until half an hour after dawn. The men would then clean their rifles at breakfast and spend the day occupied performing tasks such as sentry duty, repairing trenches, digging latrines or bringing up supplies from the stores. If fighting broke out then the men would not only have to fight back, but would also have to carry wounded soldiers to the regimental aid post. If there were no hostilities then lunch would be taken at midday and dinner would take place in the early evening. Half an hour before dusk the men would again stand on the trench fire step with their bayonets held before them and wait until half an hour after dusk before they could depart. Once darkness had fallen, wiring parties would be sent out into no man's land to repair gaps in the wire and patrols would be sent out to report on enemy activity and the state of their defences.

The former Brighton & Hove Albion goalkeeper Bob Whiting said the following about the toil in the trenches: 'I can honestly tell you it is all work and very little play. You feel a bit fatigued in the trenches after you have been there for 24 hours building up parapets, which the fellows across the way knock down with their whizzbangs.'

On 22 December 1915, having completed their first tour of duty, the battalion marched back to their billets in Beuvry to enjoy the Christmas festivities as much as they possibly could.

In order to boost morale a Christmas Eve concert was organised for the men, which one soldier described in a letter home: 'The band played sections. There were two very scratchy films (a Charlie Chaplin and a cowboy one), funny men recitations and cornet and violin solos – also songs and carols. Everything was excellent bar the air, which was as thick as a gas attack due to the Christmas smokes! It seemed very funny to think that we were only two miles away from the Germans.'

While Cardiff City had no official games during this time, they were still sporadically playing friendly matches. On 27 December 1915, during a game against Barnsley, the club organised a collection for Fred and goalkeeper John Stephenson. The match programme stated: 'It is hoped to send each of these old City favourites a parcel of comforts from time to time, and if the response is sufficiently generous, to provide refreshments for the wounded soldiers who visit Ninian Park during the season.'

In January 1916, a Cardiff City match programme explained that a 'substantial parcel' had been sent to Fred and Stephenson and that they had written to thank the club and its supporters. The programme read: 'I have seen the letters and am able to vouch for the depth of feeling contained in their expression of thanks. By the way, the optimistic note struck by both of them on the result and duration of the war was most prominently expressed. They both believe the war will end this year, while Keenor can see himself cakewalking to Berlin.'

Unfortunately, the war would last a lot longer than Fred had envisioned, and by the end of it he would be lucky to be walking at all, let alone 'cakewalking to Berlin'.

Amid the hell of life on the front line, the battalion did occasionally find time to play football, most notably in the Divisional Cup, which was a tournament played between the various Army divisions. As would be expected, the Footballers' Battalion, with players such as Fred Keenor, Vivian Woodward and Frank Buckley in the team, cruised through the early stages of the tournament with relative ease. On 11 April 1916, the battalion faced the 34th Brigade RFA in the Divisional Cup Final, winning 11–0. Fred said of the competition: 'As was only to be expected, our side carried everything before them. We were invincible. For winning the cup we received medals made of bronze which were almost as big as frying pans. As one wag suggested, they would have made good breastplates the next time we went into action.'

Woodward was not able to participate in the Final of the Divisional Cup as he had been wounded on 2 February 1916. Consequently he had been sent back to London to recuperate. Thankfully, reports in the London press that he had died proved to be premature.

The battalion may have won the Divisional Cup, but shortly afterwards it lost its first professional footballer to the war. The recruit's name was former Reading and Queen's Park Rangers player, Corporal Ben Butler. Revd Samuel Green, a chaplain, said the following of him: 'A great, big chap lies in this bed – a guard bulges up the blankets over his leg. "Well Corporal, how are you now?" – "Bad. This leg is done in. No more football for me. I'm a pro and play for –" I look at the papers and see his thigh is shattered – always dangerous, these wounds. However, the danger is not immediate and I shall have many more half-hours at this bedside. He fights for dear life for 10 days, and then goes out. He has played his last game. I doubt not he has won. A fine fellow – may he rest in peace.'

Following the Divisional Cup win, Major Frank Buckley was also wounded when shrapnel hit him in the chest and punctured his lungs. George Pyke of Newcastle United wrote: 'A stretcher party was passing the trench at the time. They asked if we had a passenger to go back. They took Major Buckley but he seemed so badly hit, you would not think he would last out as far as the Casualty Clearing Station.'

Major Buckley was subsequently sent to a military hospital in Kent to have his injuries tended to. Although he recovered, he would never be able to play football again. Displaying characteristic guts, Major Buckley returned to the Western Front in 1917, but his damaged lungs were unable to cope with the poisonous gas being used by the Germans and he was again forced to return home to recuperate.

It would not be long, however, before Fred and the rest of the battalion suffered at the hands of the war. In July 1916, the British forces were involved in a bitter battle at the Somme, an agricultural area and woodland between Peronne and the city of Amiens.

The area where the fighting was particularly ferocious was Delville Wood (also referred to as 'The Devil's Wood'), an area of woodland covering some 156 acres. On 25 July 1916, Fred and the Footballers' Battalion began their march to the Devil's Wood and were shocked by the scenes that greeted them when they finally arrived. One soldier said:

> The horrors of that ghastly place were now everywhere evident. The fearful havoc created by our barrage of the early morning, when no less than 369 guns of all calibres had poured a continuous storm of shells upon the unfortunate enemy, had piled destruction upon destruction. Branches of trees had been flung about in all directions; the thick undergrowth of the wood was pitted with shell-holes into which the enemy had crept for shelter – the whole place was in a state of indescribable confusion – to the attackers it was almost like creeping through a jungle, not knowing where the enemy was lurking or at what minute he might be encountered. The dead were everywhere – equipment littered the ground; and above all, in the momentary pauses between shell-burst and another, the moans and agonised cries of the wounded calling for water or assistance, lent a final touch to an altogether ghastly scene.

Fred would describe the Devil's Wood as a 'hellish battle', but admired his fellow recruits for displaying such bravery in horrendous conditions:

> One must pay tribute to the good work of the Footballers' Battalion. Stationed at Delville Wood, Jerry's artillery threw everything he had at us – and then some. It simply rained shells. The wonder was that any of us came out alive.
>
> It was attack and counter-attack day and night, but during the battle for possession of this wood there was not a sign of cowardice among

our men. Some of them may have been called 'windy' on the football fields of England, but out there in France they stood the real test of all.

With shells and artillery being fired at him from all angles, Fred was wounded when shrapnel penetrated his leg just above his knee. Fred tried to get up and walk, but his injured leg collapsed underneath him. As he lay amid the carnage, with blood seeping from his thigh, he must have wondered whether he would survive. Mercifully a fellow soldier spotted Fred trying to crawl to safety and helped him escape. Without this unnamed soldier's assistance the fortunes of Cardiff City and Welsh football could have turned out to be very different.

On inspection Fred's leg wound appeared so severe that doctors felt that it would spell the end of his football career, and there were even fears that the limb might need to be amputated. After spending six months in a Dublin hospital, where he went through agonising rehabilitation work, Fred made a full recovery – but he would carry the physical and emotional scars with him for the rest of his life.

In the years that followed the war, Fred's son, Graham, revealed that Fred was not comfortable reminiscing about the atrocities that he had witnessed, when he said:

He never liked to discuss anything to do with the war. The only reference I can ever remember him making was to Delville Wood in the Battle of the Somme, which was being held by the South Africans. It came under a terrific barrage and went up like a massive bonfire. There was a relic of the war because I noticed Dad had an indentation in his right shoulder – as if someone had gouged out a piece from underneath his right shoulder blade. I don't know if they left the shrapnel in there or not. He wouldn't be drawn on it. I found him most reluctant to discuss it. The impression I got was that the war was so horrendous that, along with a great many other soldiers, Dad blotted it out. He had lost too many friends. He often said that he was one of the lucky ones who came back. As well as his shoulder, he also damaged his knees, but none of the injuries seemed to affect him. He was very fit and as strong as an ox. He obviously sustained that right through his career.

Fred's injuries were painful, but they paled in comparison to the fate of some of his comrades. William Jonas, of Clapton Orient, was one such unlucky individual who lost his life during the hostilities. Jonas's teammate, CSM McFadden, was in a trench with him shortly before his death and he wrote of Jonas's final moments:

> Both Willie and I were trapped in a trench...Willie turned to me and said, 'Goodbye Mac. Best of luck, special love to my sweetheart Mary Jane and best regards to the lads at Orient.' Before I could reply to him he was up and over. No sooner had he jumped out of the trench, my best friend of nearly 20 years was killed before my eyes.

In regard to the fate of the Cardiff City recruits, both Tom Witts and Ken McKenzie were killed in action, as was Lord Ninian Crichton-Stuart. Goalkeeper John Stephenson survived the war but was so severely wounded that he would never play football again. Men who had given so much to their football club had now made the ultimate sacrifice for their country.

It was not, however, all doom and gloom, as in 1917 Cardiff City trainer George Latham, who had already fought in the Boer War (1899–1902), was awarded the Military Cross for bravery for his efforts when fighting in the Middle East. A Cardiff City match programme would reveal just how highly regarded Latham was at the club, for his achievements and general disposition:

> While we admire him for his football achievements, and still more for his lofty patriotism, we find still more to attract us in his smiling and genial disposition, in his unfailing courtesy, and in his self-sacrificing and sympathetic heart.

It is men like Latham whose example has been a beacon to the race, whose conduct has fulfilled the highest aspirations of human endeavour, whose deeds will echo through the corridor of time.

For the remainder of the war, Fred Keenor was based in Chatham, where he served as a fitness instructor. In May 1917, Fred's war efforts were recognised when he was promoted from the rank of Private to Sergeant Corporal. He was also awarded the Victory Medal, the 1914–15 Star and the British War Medal.

Being stationed in Chatham provided Fred with the opportunity to play for Brentford, whom he said had 'a fine side and put all the big clubs around London in the shade'. In one game against Fulham, Fred arrived at Craven Cottage an hour early only to find around 20 well-known internationals waiting to see if they could get a game. Fred recalled that one of his teammates said of the prospect of facing this all-star team: 'Blimey, they may as well have advertised this as Brentford vs All England'.

Despite the strength of the Fulham team, Brentford won the game and went on to win the London Combination Championship.

The war eventually came to an end on 11 November 1918 when Germany surrendered. Over the course of the conflict the British Empire had mobilised nearly nine million men and women for war service and had suffered over three million casualties. It is estimated that around 900 men who served in the Footballers' Battalion lost their lives; many others were left maimed and/or traumatised.

Major Buckley kept a record of what happened to the men who had been under his command during the war. He later wrote that by the mid-1930s over 500 of the 600 men he was in charge of were dead.

As the war came to a close some struggled to adapt to civilian life; however, as always, life continued and there were calls for football to resume. Many who had played professional football just four years previously would not be around to take part.

CHAPTER 4

GETTING BACK TO NORMALITY

Season 1919–20

Following the war, Fred returned to Cardiff and looked forward to resuming his football career. However, the Southern League had still not set a date when it would recommence and as a result Fred was forced to find temporary work in a gasworks, and on a milk round, in order to make ends meet.

At this time Fred also started a relationship with an attractive girl by the name of Muriel Griffiths. Muriel had worked in a munitions factory during the war, but she was also a very accomplished musician and played the organ in a church in her home town of Swansea.

Fred was besotted with the petite but feisty brunette, especially as she was one of the few girls who would stand her ground with him. After a whirlwind romance Fred and Muriel got married on 11 November 1919. Once they were married the pair were eager to start a family, and they welcomed their first child, Frederick, to the world in May 1920.

Prior to getting married, however, Fred finally returned to his career as a professional footballer in August 1919. Cardiff City would be back playing in the First Division of the Southern League and were in the relatively fortunate position of having not lost too many of their squad to the war.

Over the course of the war years the Cardiff manager, Fred Stewart, had remained in the city running a coal merchant's business. He was now eager to get back to football and set about building a team that could challenge for the title.

The financial situation at Ninian Park was still dire, as the club had only received limited income during the war years due to the team playing just a handful of friendly games in front of poor crowds. The directors of Cardiff City had kept the club afloat with money out of their own pockets, and without their help the club would surely not have survived.

Notwithstanding the tight purse strings, the directors gave Stewart some money with which to purchase new recruits. His first post-war signing was Bradford City's Billy Grimshaw, whom Cardiff bought for £1,000. He also signed former Manchester United player Arthur Cashmore, who would finish the forthcoming season as the side's top goalscorer with 14 goals in just 22 games.

Stewart had the war itself to thank for one of his other signings. Ernest 'Bert' Smith had met some of the Cardiff players while fighting in France and had been advised to go to Ninian Park for a trial. The trial was a success and Smith became an integral and popular member of Stewart's team, as he hilariously claimed that he could mesmerise opponents by staring into their faces! Fred recalled one incident in which Smith supposedly put this talent to good use: 'In one game we lost one man through injury and things were not going too well for us. In fact, we were a couple of goals down when our opponents were awarded a penalty. As this was about to be taken Bert turned to me and said, "Watch him miss it Fred." True enough the kicker, who was known as a "penalty king", missed the target by a good yard. "It's a pity you did not think of that before they scored the other goals!" I said to him.'

Before the war, Fred had been a bit-part player but now, four years on, at the age of 25 and with the experience of playing for the Footballers' Battalion and Brentford behind him, he was ready to become a major influence for both club and country. The *South Wales Football Echo* also noted the improvement in Fred's ability following the war: 'Keenor may be said to have had his opportunity of gaining first-class experience by the accident of the war. Keenor during that period played for Brentford and improved to such an extent during the time he was associated with that club that his selection in Cardiff City's team this season was practically assured.'

In pre-season Fred featured in two out of the three friendly games that Cardiff played, with both his appearances coming against Bristol City. His performances in those friendly games gave Fred Stewart a selection dilemma. Pat Cassidy usually played in Fred's position of right-half and was a highly accomplished player himself; however, in a selfless act, Cassidy pushed forward Fred's case for him to start in the team ahead of him. As reported in the *South Wales Football Echo*: 'Keenor some time ago stood a chance of losing his position through the introduction of Cassidy, but to the latter's credit, be it said, no one more strongly objected to the change then he himself, and he appealed to the directors to continue playing Keenor on the ground that the Welsh international had youth on his side and was full of promise.'

Following his impressive pre-season performances, and Cassidy's plea, Fred played in Cardiff's opening League fixture against Reading. While the team lost the game 2–0, Fred delivered an accomplished display.

With Fred still in the team, Cardiff won their first game of the season on 6 September 1919, beating Southampton 3–0. Fred even managed to get himself on the score sheet in what turned out to be a successful day for club and player.

Having missed four years of football due to the war, there seemed to be a significant increase in interest in the game throughout Wales as people were no doubt desperate to put the misery of the war years behind them. An example of this was seen when Cardiff and Swansea clashed at the Vetch Field on 27 September 1919. The *South Wales Football Echo* reported: 'If evidence was required to prove that Association has obtained a grip of the sporting public in South Wales, that the game is booming, and that the enthusiasm is far greater this year than it has ever previously been, it was supplied on Saturday, when the holding up of the train service caused difficulty in transport that would have dampened the ardour of football followers who were not keen enthusiasts. Yet there were more than 15,000 spectators at the Vetch Field, Swansea, on the occasion of Cardiff City's visit.'

Cardiff lost out to their bitter rivals 2–1, but soon had another derby game to contest against Newport County at Somerton Park. On this occasion Cardiff emerged victorious in a hard-fought 1–3 win. Once more the *South Wales Football Echo* reported on the game and provided an insight into how football had captivated the Welsh public following a number of poorly-attended rugby games: 'Pioneers of Association Football in South Wales have reason to rejoice over the amount of interest now taken in the game. The hope of years gone by has been more than realised, and it is doubtful whether the most ardent enthusiast of those days when the dribbling code was striving hard to gain a footing in rugby centres would have ventured to predict that in a comparatively short period Soccer would do more than hold its own against all opposition. This season's experience has shown that there is room in South Wales for the two codes, but it is surely strong evidence in support of the contention that soccer has now obtained a grip that will enable it to win through.'

Shortly afterwards Portsmouth visited Ninian Park and the press again were left to marvel at football's popularity in the Principality: 'English clubs making their first appearance in South Wales since pre-war days marvel at the increased popularity of the game in the lower half of the Principality. Local enthusiasts who have watched the growth of the game were not unprepared for the rapid advancement, but it is doubtful whether even local supporters were not agreeably surprised in learning that despite a counter attraction in the form of Cardiff Races, a record gate witnessed the match at Ninian Park.'

Cardiff were by now well into their stride, and following their loss to Swansea only tasted defeat once in their next 23 games. At one stage the team even looked favourites to win the title, but unfortunately it was not to be, as in the final stages of the season the team dramatically collapsed and only managed to win three of their last 12 games. Regardless of this, the team still managed to finish in a credible fourth position, but they were left frustrated at letting the title slip from their grasp.

The team did manage to win a trophy that season, however, when they won the Welsh Cup for just the second time in the club's short history, when Wrexham were defeated 2–1 in the Welsh Cup Final.

Fred would add further silverware to his collection as his performances for Cardiff City caught the eye of the Welsh national team selectors. Owing to an injury to Jennings of Bolton, a fiercely proud Fred was subsequently selected to make his international debut in the Welsh side's Victory International against England. Fred put in an impressive performance in the 2–0 win, but it was still expected that he would lose his place in the next international game when Jennings would be fit to play; however, this was not to be the case, as the *South Wales Football Echo* reported: 'Keenor indeed created a very fine impression, and notwithstanding the announcement that Bolton would consent to Jennings taking part in the game it came as a surprise that the Selection Committee made it known that Keenor was not to be displaced.'

In his first season as an international, Fred made the position of right-half his own, as Wales famously won the Victory Shield for the first time.

Fred made a total of 43 appearances for Cardiff City in the League and Cup over the season as well as becoming a Welsh international. He had at last become a permanent fixture in the team and would remain so until he finally left the club in 1931. Over the course of the season Fred was described in the local press as a 'barbarian', a 'viking' and as a 'trojan', such were his action-packed performances in both defence and attack.

However, one phrase that would not be used to describe Fred was 'good looking'. With his long face, crooked teeth, protruding ears and large nose, Fred was certainly not a handsome man – as he himself admitted: 'I was never what the ladies call a "good looker".'

During the season the players decided to play a match where the best-looking players took on the worst. While it is not documented which team Fred represented, it is safe to assume that he was not a member of the best-looking players' side:

It is generally known that the City players pride themselves on their good looks. Wherever they got the idea from Heaven only knows, but there it is.

Somebody suggested that a match should be played by the 11 best-looking players versus the rest. Then the trouble started. 'Kidder'

Harvey asserted that he ought to head the list of Beauties! And was deeply hurt when Jack Evans suggested that he looked like the Wreck of the *Hesperus*.

But when Pat Cassidy claimed the right to appear in the Adonis class, the comments on his facial appearance were most rude. George West said he wasn't much to look at ('Hear hear') but whatever happened, he didn't want to appear in the same class as Kneeshaw, who replied that he wasn't a candidate for the dogs home. In his opinion, Nature had perpetrated one of her worst jokes when she turned out West. (They don't speak now.)

When George Beare claimed a right to appear in the same side as Charlie Brittan (who by general consent was given his place in the side), Layton told him in the most forceful manner that whatever side Beare was in, he wished to be on the other, as he wasn't risking his reputation for good looks by playing with the outside-right.

The voting is expected to be interesting and exciting. The only certainties appear to be Brittan and Smith. The lavish offers of cigarettes, one to the other, bears somewhat the semblance of bribery and there seems no other way to account for their humility and apparent courtesy to each other.

The team spirit in the side was obviously a good one and this had no doubt contributed to Cardiff's success that season. With the team performing admirably crowds had flocked to Ninian Park, which meant that attendances had been in the region of 20,000. The increased gates helped strengthen the club's troubled finances and as a result it could afford to improve the facilities at Ninian Park.

One of the first objectives for the directors was to increase the capacity at the stadium in order to provide more income. They therefore decided to build an all-seater Canton Stand that would not only increase capacity, but would also provide a more comfortable area for fans to sit in. Slowly but surely Cardiff City was being transformed from an amateur team who played on a rubbish tip to an ambitious, youthful team who were going places.

An interesting side note to the season occurred when, in October 1919, the legendary Cardiff boxer, 'Peerless' Jim Driscoll (the former World Featherweight Champion), trained at Ninian Park in order to prepare for a clash against Frenchman Charles Ledoux.

Fred Keenor was a fanatical boxing fan and looked forward to seeing one of his heroes at close quarters. As a fitness instructor in the army Fred had enjoyed boxing in various army competitions. He won more bouts than he lost and at one point considered taking the sport up seriously, until one day he fought an opponent who was a stone heavier than him. Despite this disadvantage Fred typically did not back down and said, 'although I knew I was in for a hiding I went in to do or die'. However, in the third round of the fight Fred recalled that his opponent 'must have hit me with the roof' and as a result he was knocked out. After this experience Fred's interest in boxing came to an end.

The opportunity, however, to get in the ring with 'Peerless' while he was training at Ninian Park proved too much for Fred to resist, as he was keen to see how he would fare against the former World Featherweight Champion. Even though 'Peerless' was 14 years older than Fred, and Fred had previous boxing experience, he never managed to lay a glove on the veteran boxer, such was his ability. Fred said of the bout: 'I do not think I hit him once, but I can still feel the piston-rod left landing on my flattened nose. They were just light taps. Jim was not the sort of man to take advantage, but he proved to me that I did the right thing in announcing that I had retired as a boxer for all time.'

Unfortunately, 'Peerless' lost his fight against Ledoux in what would turn out to be the last fight in his fantastic career. When 'Peerless' died in 1925, Fred, along with many of Cardiff's players and officials, was among the estimated 100,000 people who attended his funeral. Such is the devotion of the Cardiff public to 'Peerless' Jim Driscoll that a statute was erected in his honour, more than 75 years after his death.

Cardiff's campaign had been a success, but the best news was still yet to come. Midway through the season news had broken that the Football League intended to create a new Third Division, which would be in place for the 1920–21 season. It was envisioned that the Third Division would mainly consist of Southern League First Division clubs, of which Cardiff was one.

On 6 March 1920, the *South Wales Football Echo* informed Cardiff City supporters that the club had applied for admission to the Third Division of the Football League:

> There is a possibility of South Wales figuring still more prominently in the football world, and if the ambitious scheme of Cardiff City is realised enthusiasts in the lower half of the Principality will be brought into direct touch with a competition that in the course of time will enable them to see at Cardiff the leading teams in the country taking part in the season's programme. Small wonder it is, therefore, that the followers of the Association code, not only in the Welsh Metropolis itself, but in the outlying districts, express their delight at the step taken by Cardiff City directors.
>
> This matter of applying for admission into the Third Division of the English League has long been considered by the City directorate, but it was only a week ago that they decided to make known their intention to do so, and if they are able to do more towards popularising the game in South Wales than has already been done through their successful achievement in the Southern League and FA Cup.

Cardiff's application may have initially only been for admittance into the Third Division, but such was the quality of their application that the Football League opted to place the club into the Second Division. This was a highly controversial decision, as Portsmouth, who had won the Southern League First Division title that year, remained in the bottom tier.

In later years Fred said of Cardiff's election to the Football League: 'I shall always contend that it was only through the untiring efforts of Fred Stewart, secretary-manager of the club, and the helpful publicity of the Cardiff press, that Cardiff achieved their objective.'

Fred recalled that on the morning of the meeting of the Football League, when they would decide whether Cardiff would be admitted, that every member present was furnished with a copy of the *Western Mail*, which outlined the numerous benefits of having Cardiff in the League. Quite obviously the wartime spats between the club and the newspaper had been long forgotten.

While Cardiff were admitted to the Second Division of the Football League, at the same time Swansea Town, Newport County, Aberdare Athletic and Merthyr Town were admitted to the new Third Division South and Wrexham to the Third Division North. Wales therefore went from having no teams in the Football League to having six. This would be the zenith of Welsh participation in the Football League.

Cardiff City was the highest-placed Welsh side in the Football League and Fred did not feel that the club was only representing the people of Cardiff, he also felt that it was representing Wales as a whole. He said: 'We had made up our minds that, come what may, we'd do our best to shine and show England that Wales could run a big club successfully.'

The forthcoming season would be the start of an exciting adventure for Cardiff City as they looked forward to life in the country's premier football competition, the Football League.

Season 1920–21

With the thrill of Cardiff City entering the Football League came the realisation that the team would need to be significantly strengthened if it was going to be competitive. Fred Stewart, a master in the transfer market and an outstanding judge of a player, consequently made 13 new signings before the season had begun. One of his most notable signings was that of Jimmy Gill from Sheffield Wednesday, who was bought for the sum of £750. Fred was a huge fan of Gill's and said that he 'could do anything with the ball except make it sit up and talk'.

Some notable names did leave Ninian Park that summer, however, when two of the 'holy three' were released: 'Kidder' Harvey and Pat Cassidy. Stewart was obviously comfortable in the knowledge that Fred was a more than able replacement for these former Cardiff heroes and felt no need to retain them.

As a result Fred once more started the season in the Cardiff side as they began life in the Football League with an away fixture against Stockport County. Stockport was ironically the club where Fred Stewart had spent 18 years as manager before joining Cardiff City. Cardiff announced their intent for the season, and thrilled their supporters in the process, by winning the game 5–2. Fred scored Cardiff's all-important third goal in what was a dream Football League debut.

Following this fine opening-day victory Cardiff were in menacing form, losing only once in their first 12 games. One of those games was a 3–0 win over Fulham, which saw Fred score again: 'Keenor gained great applause for a very clever bit of work bringing off a sparkling run – winding up his effort with a fine and accurate drive that beat the defence.'

With the team marching towards the top of the division, and attendances regularly hitting 25,000, Fred Stewart was provided with further funds in order to strengthen the team. He subsequently spent a club record fee of £3,500 on Sheffield Wednesday's Scottish international full-back Jimmy Blair.

The introduction of Blair into the Cardiff team ensured that they continued with their winning streak when they defeated Bristol City 1–0 in front of 43,000 fans at Ninian Park. Even though the Cardiff defence looked impregnable, scoring goals was becoming an issue. In order to address this problem Fred Stewart was provided with further funds so that he could purchase Harry Nash from Coventry City and Fred Pagnam from Arsenal. Both players would get on the score sheet on their debuts and go on to score vital goals for the side during the remainder of the season.

After the team's dramatic collapse at the end of the 1919–20 season, the players were mindful that this time around they must not lose focus. Accordingly, in the final 11 games of the season the team was magnificent and lost only once. During this spell the defence, which included Fred within its ranks, went six consecutive matches without conceding a goal; however, the one game that Cardiff did lose, 2–0 away to Hull, would ultimately prove costly, as despite Cardiff beating Wolves 3–1 in the last game of the season, they just missed out on the title to Birmingham City by virtue of an inferior goal difference.

In an interview Fred recalled the agony of failing to win the title, and how difficult it was to calculate the all-important goal difference in the days before Sky Sports and calculators: 'Having beaten Wolverhampton in our last game, we waited anxiously in the dressing room for the result of the Birmingham match. It seemed hours before the result came through. We were level on points. Out came pencils and paper, and a dozen or so amateur mathematicians tried to work out the percentages. First we were on top, then we were not, and this went on for at least 15 minutes, when a reporter walked in with the information that Birmingham were champions. Their goal average was a tiny fraction of one per cent better than ours.'

Regardless of losing out on the title to Birmingham the team was still promoted to the First Division. This was a remarkable achievement considering it was Cardiff's first season in the Football League.

Cardiff's success that season was not limited to the League, as the team also reached the semi-final of the FA Cup. Yet before reaching that stage of the competition the team had to overcome some formidable obstacles, most notably Sunderland in front of a ferocious crowd at Roker Park. The press said of Cardiff's famous victory in the North East: 'Judged by the number of congratulatory messages received by Mr Fred Stewart, Cardiff City's secretary-manager, no other victory in the Cup competition could prove more popular than that gained by the Cardiffians, and in addition to the pleasure the team's achievements has given to their supporters it is doubtful whether any other performance of the day is considered by football enthusiasts far removed from the vicinity of the Taff to equal in merit that of the conquerors of the famous Sunderland organisation.'

In the following rounds Cardiff faced, and saw off, Brighton and Southampton, before having to play Chelsea in the quarter-final. The Welsh public had been captivated by Cardiff's Cup run, and in the lead up to the match the hype surrounding the game reached fever pitch.

Such was the pressure on the team at Ninian Park that Fred recalled that for the first 10 minutes of the match all of the players seemed overawed by the occasion and struggled to get going; however, the Bluebirds did finally settle and after 30 minutes Cashmore scored the game's only goal, which was enough to send Cardiff City into the semi-finals of the FA Cup.

Cardiff were drawn to play fellow Second Division side Wolverhampton Wanderers in the semi-final and thus fancied their chances of progressing to the Final. The game, which was played at Anfield, was a cagey affair with neither team going for the jugular. It was of no surprise that the game ended scoreless. History was made, as King George V and Queen Mary watched the game and thus became the first reigning monarchs to attend a football match.

The exciting replay at Old Trafford, just four days later, was an altogether different affair to the dire first match. Wolves rocketed into an early two-goal lead thanks to some debatable refereeing decisions, and the Bluebirds were at one point in real danger of being humiliated.

With the score still 2–0, Cardiff were awarded a penalty. Despite the fact that there were forwards of the calibre of Jimmy Gill on the field, the team looked to Fred to take on the responsibility of taking the pressure kick. Fred held his nerve and scored the penalty to make the score 2–1; however, Cardiff's fightback was in vain as Wolves went on to score a third goal, which was enough to knock the Bluebirds out of the FA Cup. To top off a disappointing day Fred also received two black eyes after getting hit in the face by a stray elbow.

The murkier side of professional football also crossed paths with Fred during the season when he was asked whether he was interested in a bribe before a game. Fred recalled:

One day I was stopped by a well dressed individual: 'Hullo Fred' he said as if he had known me for years although he was a complete stranger, 'how are you going to fare today?'

Naturally I replied that I thought we should win, but imagine my surprise when he told me that if it was made worth his while he would 'arrange' the match so that the points would be ours.

A certain player was mentioned as being 'in the swindle'.

Fred was too proud a man to even consider authorising the backhander and duly told the man that neither he nor his team were interested. Ironically, the Bluebirds played the game and lost, with the opposing player alleged to be 'in the swindle' scoring two of his team's goals. Fred felt that it was his duty to report the incident and subsequently informed the authorities, but no action was ever taken.

In spite of the heartbreaking semi-final loss, and just missing out on the title, the team had excelled in its first season in the Football League. Record attendances had also meant that the club's finances were for once in rude health. Cardiff's exciting style of play was also recognised throughout the country and the *South Wales Football Echo* heralded the team's brand of football: 'In all parts of the country Cardiff City is described as the team of the year, and surely no other club has a better right to be so designated. Some of their performances have been really brilliant, and as a source of attraction they have been placed right in the forefront.'

Charlie Brittan's father, who was a builder in Portsmouth, was so proud of his son's achievements during the season that he named a street of houses that he had built in the Hampshire naval port, Ninian Park Road. The street still exists to this day and it is situated not too far away from Portsmouth's Fratton Park stadium.

The team had every right to feel optimistic as it reached the big time of British football, the First Division of the Football League.

Season 1921–22

In the summer of 1921 both Fred and Cardiff City were busy adding new bodies to their respective families. Muriel Keenor gave birth to a second child, Gladys, and Fred Stewart scoured the country for suitable players to add to his squad.

Such was Stewart's unbridled enthusiasm to improve his team that he was even fined £50 for making an illegal approach to Waugh of Wolves. It goes to show that the 'tapping up' of players is not just a modern-day phenomenon. Despite this setback Stewart still managed to make nine signings, which included the capture of Jack Rutherford, who was informed of his transfer by wireless while he was on a ship crossing the Atlantic.

On 27 August 1921, Cardiff City kicked-off the season with a glamour match against FA Cup-holders Tottenham Hotspur at Ninian Park. There was such interest in the game that three hours before kick-off queues stretched around the ground. The turnstiles eventually had to be closed when the official capacity of 50,000 was reached. Some of the disappointed fans outside the stadium were so desperate to see the game that they forced open the exit gates in order to gain entry. In the end it is estimated that between 55–60,000 fans were crammed into Ninian Park as supporters even sat on the scoreboard due to the lack of space in the stands.

Unfortunately, not only did Cardiff lose the opening game 1–0 to Tottenham, but they also tasted defeat in the following five games. Regardless of the poor start to the season, Fred was not daunted by the step up in class: 'It was not a good start, but we were not discouraged, and really believed that once we had sensed the finer touch of First Division football we would do better.'

The team finally recorded their first win of the season when they beat Middlesbrough 3–1 in front of 50,000 giddy fans at Ninian Park. Ironically, Middlesbrough were the League leaders at the time, while Cardiff were rock bottom.

Winning against the League leaders, and in such an emphatic fashion, was rapturously received by the Cardiff fans, who were so eager for success. The *South Wales Football Echo* commented: 'It was more than a mere win, it was a triumph, and one of the keenest followers of the team said at the close of the match: "It was worth being defeated in the earlier games to have this opportunity of showing how we appreciate our team." The consensus of opinion was that the game equalled the previous best-ever seen on the ground.'

The game was not just notable for the surprise victory; it was also a turning point in Fred's career. Fred's usual position in the team was right-half, but for this game he was selected to play at centre-half. Fred Stewart had always been reluctant to play Keenor in the centre, due to his lack of height, but on the occasions when he had played there he had always performed well. Fred did not let his manager down as he delivered a composed, intelligent, wholehearted display, and as a result of this performance he spent the remainder of his career playing primarily in the centre.

One of Fred's teammates, Herbie Evans, commented on how well Fred adapted to his new position after the Middlesbrough game: 'Fred never looked back after that. He used to dominate the centre of the field. He was absolutely fearless, very strong in the tackle and good in the air, although he wasn't a particularly tall man.'

Fred continued to earn praise for his performances in his new position and he was especially keen to play well against Bolton, where he would come face to face with Jennings, his adversary for his place in the Wales team. Jennings was said to have played well but it was to be Cardiff City's and Fred's day as they won 2–I. The *South Wales Football Echo* said of Fred's performance: 'At half-back, Keenor again proved that he was an able pivot. He opened the game delightfully.'

It was not just Fred who was enjoying a fine run of form, however; with Smith and Hardy injured, two local amateurs from Cardiff, Herbie Evans and Eddie Jenkins, were brought into the side to play alongside Fred at right-half and left-half. The Cardiff trio subsequently earned rave reviews for their endeavours in the half-back line: 'There is one department of the City team that still stands out prominently – the half-back line; it is good fortune for the Cardiffians that they have discovered not only the two clever amateurs to make up the line but also a centre-half who bids fair to make a name in the position. He dominated the play; he distributed passes so judiciously that the opponents were frequently taken by surprise, and had no opportunity to tumble to his style of play.'

And: 'Time after time have the City directors been given cause to congratulate themselves upon the fund of talent that they have at their disposal. When they had such men as Smith and Hardy down they discovered that a reorganized back line, with Keenor in the centre supported by H.P. Evans and Eddie Jenkins, was strong enough for any team in the country.'

By the time Fred had finally found his natural position in the Cardiff team he had unbelievably been at the club for 10 years. The club subsequently arranged a testimonial match for him against Bristol City. In the match programme for the game Fred answered some questions about himself in his typical forthright manner:

Favourite position? *Any old where.*
Favourite motto? *Live and Learn.*
When do you feel at your best? *When everything goes right.*
Greatest ambition? *To play as long as Billy Meredith.*
Pet aversion? *Unfair critics.*
Favourite hobby? *Gardening.*
Which is your lucky day? *Pay day.*

Not long after the testimonial game Fred came up against the 48-year-old Billy Meredith in a game against Manchester City at Ninian Park; however, it was not Meredith who caught the eye that day, rather it was the performance of the Manchester City captain and centre-half Max Woosnam that received all the plaudits. The *South Wales Football Echo* said: 'Two men stood out in the Manchester team. They were Blair, the goalkeeper, and Max Woosnam, the great amateur centre-half. The latter was a dominating force both in attack and defence.'

Max Woosnam is perhaps the greatest sportsman in history, as he excelled at so many different sports. As a schoolboy he scored 144 runs for a Public Schools XI cricket team while playing against the MCC at Lord's. He attended Cambridge University where he played football, cricket, tennis and golf, becoming a quadruple Cambridge Blue in the process. He won a doubles title at Wimbledon, captained the Great Britain Davis Cup tennis team and won an Olympic gold medal in tennis. He also turned down the opportunity to captain the Great Britain football team at the Olympics, but still went on to captain England and Manchester City. As well as being a scratch golfer, and achieving a maximum 147 break at snooker, he also famously beat Charlie Chaplin at table tennis, playing with a butter knife instead of a bat.

Cardiff lost to Max Woosnam's Manchester City that day and their form remained inconsistent in subsequent games. One player who was consistent, however, was forward Jimmy Gill, who was running riot. After scoring two goals in the win against Middlesbrough, Gill then scored a further seven goals in the next seven games. Unfortunately, Gill's besieged strike partner, Len Pagnam, who had only signed for Cardiff the previous season, was struggling, and at one point went 14 games without registering a goal. Indeed, the *South Wales Football Echo* said of Pagnam's goalless streak: 'The most striking feature in connection with the forward line is the failure of Pagnam to get goals. He is the most unfortunate player in the side in this respect, because he has come so near to doing the trick and has actually netted on three occasions only to have the scores disallowed.'

Pagnam's miserable form was enough to persuade Fred Stewart to again dive into the transfer market and spend £1,500 on Everton forward Joe Clennell. In order to recoup some of this money Arthur Cashmore was transferred to Notts County and the hapless Pagnam was sold to Watford.

Clennell made an immediate impact at the club and between 12 November 1921 and 25 February 1922 Cardiff only lost one game and shot up the table. But Fred was one of the casualties from the side during this winning streak, due to firstly obtaining an injury and then catching a bad dose of flu. While Fred was out of the side a Cardiff City match programme reported: 'It is a matter of regret that Keenor is still unable to play. He has contracted a severe cold which has laid him so low that he may not be able to turn out for a few weeks.'

When Fred did return the fact that he was still suffering with illness and injury, coupled with the stellar performance of the Cardiff half-back line, meant that he had few opportunities to play. Obviously frustrated with having missed three years of his career due to the war, and being regarded as one of the best defenders in the country, Fred went to see the Cardiff directors and asked for a transfer. Mercifully the directors persuaded Fred to stay and fight for his place.

On 14 January 1922, Fred eventually returned to the side when he was asked to deputise at inside-right as Cardiff beat Birmingham City 3–1. Yet while Fred played well, it was apparent to everyone that he was still not fully fit: 'That

Keenor did so well at inside-right is a tribute to his versatility, but there were many times that he gave evidence of having been affected by his recent illness.'

For the rest of the season Fred was in and out of the side as he battled against various injuries and tried to build up his stamina following his severe bout of flu.

During this time one of the more amusing stories in the history of Cardiff City occurred when Cardiff faced Blackburn Rovers at Ewood Park. Just before the game Jimmy Gill and Jack Evans went down with flu and were unable to play. Only one reserve had travelled with the team to Blackburn, Harry Nash, so Cardiff were still one player short. The team's trainer, ex-Welsh international George Latham, subsequently stepped forward and at the age of 42 became the club's oldest-ever player.

With Latham huffing and puffing around the pitch Cardiff still went on to win the game 3–1; indeed, Cardiff were in such a comfortable position that the players were able to have a little fun at Latham's expense. Knowing that Latham was tiring, yet still eager to give his all, the players began purposely hitting long passes for him to chase. Latham said: 'When we were three up, I moved to outside-right and then the lads had a game with me. They sent long forward passes to my side of the field and shouted to me to go after the ball, just to see if I had any wind left – I hadn't much.'

After the game the *South Wales Football Echo* reported on Cardiff's injury predicament and on Latham's performance:

> What an awkward situation presented itself; yet, while many a joke was cracked upon the call upon George Latham's services, every regular player in the side realised that in him they at least had a trier possessed of perfect knowledge of the game, even though his day as a first-class footballer had passed. They fielded with determination for George's sake, as they put it – and the remarkable feature of the whole game was that Latham, who had first been capped for Wales as far back as 1905, when he played against England and Scotland, fitted in so perfectly with the general scheme of things that he was a success. The popular trainer

almost scored – had he done so I'm sure his colleagues would have carried him off the field shoulder high, and at the close of the match, when he immediately set to work as usual in rubbing down his 'boys' he was wreathed in smiles as he kept repeating, 'This is the proudest moment of my life'. He is idolised by the players – he deserves to – for there can be no other trainer more keenly alert in getting his men fit.

Following the team's poor early season form they had recovered well and would finish in the comfort of fourth place. The team's performances were so vastly improved that they even beat the League champions, Liverpool, 2–0 at Ninian Park. If it had not been for the team's dismal start to the season they might even have been challenging for the title.

Over the course of the campaign Cardiff had also enjoyed another fine run in the FA Cup. In the early rounds of the competition they beat Manchester United at Old Trafford 4–2, before putting Southampton and Nottingham Forest to the sword.

For the second consecutive season, Cardiff had again reached the quarter-final stage, but would have to overcome Cup-holders Tottenham Hotspur if they wanted to progress to the semi-finals. Fred would later say that Cardiff's games against Spurs were always 'stirring' affairs and that 'whether it was in a Cup or League the match was worth going miles to see'.

The game at Ninian Park was a 'ding-dong battle', which ended in a 1–1 draw, with Len Davies grabbing a last-minute equaliser. Fred felt that Davies's goal 'must have been worth a £1,000 to the club'.

Just days after the Ninian Park clash Cardiff travelled to White Hart Lane for the replay. Fred was astonished at just how much interest there was in the game, as 'it seemed that there were more people outside the ground than inside'.

Unfortunately, Cardiff went on to lose the replay in controversial circumstances as the winning goal was scored after the Cardiff goalkeeper had been poleaxed by one of the Spurs players. The Cardiff team argued in vain that their goalkeeper had been charged into the net before the ball had reached him, but the referee was unmoved and the Bluebirds were out of the Cup.

Cardiff were, however, to enjoy greater fortune in the Welsh Cup when they again won the competition, courtesy of a 2–0 win over Ton Pentre in the Final.

The season was also notable for the signing of one of Cardiff City's most celebrated players when, in February 1922, Fred Stewart signed Irish goalkeeper Tom Farquharson from Welsh League side Abertillery.

Farquharson made his debut for Cardiff City in a 3–1 win over Manchester United on the last day of the season and went on to play 521 games for the club up until 1935. He was not only a magnificent servant, but also highly regarded for his skill in goal. Fred himself said that Farquharson was 'one of the finest goalkeepers Cardiff City ever had'.

The Irish goalkeeper's arrival in South Wales is also one of the more obscure stories in the history of Cardiff City Football Club. As a young man living in Ireland, Farquharson had helped run messages for the IRA when it was engaged in a guerrilla war (1919–21) against British Forces. Farquharson and his friend Sean Lemass (who eventually became Prime Minister of the Irish Republic from 1959 to 1966) were eventually arrested by British Forces for removing posters appealing for the whereabouts of prominent IRA members. The two were subsequently detained in Dublin's notorious Mountjoy Prison for questioning.

Farquharson's father negotiated his release from the prison on the condition that the 19-year-old left Ireland immediately. Therefore, in late 1920, the tall teenager travelled to Monmouthshire's Sirhowy Valley, where he had contacts, and started work as a carpenter.

During his time in Ireland, Farquharson had played Gaelic football, and as its nearest equivalent in South Wales was rugby union, he began playing for Blackwood Rugby Club. However, one day the local football team, Oakdale, was short of a goalkeeper and Farquharson volunteered his services, despite having never previously played the game. Regardless of his inexperience he proved such a success that Welsh League club Abertillery signed him up, and this move would eventually see Farquharson sign for Cardiff City.

Various rumours still persist that Farquharson carried a handgun with him at all times; indeed, former Cardiff player Eddie Jenkins recalled an incident in which Farquharson was arguing with full-back George Russell in 1932 and said: 'George was showing off in the dressing room one day and Tom brought out this revolver and threatened to shoot him if he didn't behave.'

Farquharson may have had a reputation for being a loose cannon, but this did not deter Fred from grabbing him by the throat and shaking him roughly in one game against Blackpool, after he had been chipped from the halfway line. Fred was so enraged by Farquharson's lapse in concentration that he continued to deliver a tirade of abuse at the 'keeper for 10 minutes afterwards.

With Farquharson in goal, a defence consisting of Billy Hardy and Fred Keenor, and a forward line of Jimmy Gill and Len Davies, the Cardiff side was confidently looking forward to the 1922–23 season.

Season 1922–23

In the summer of 1922, Fred Stewart was so confident in the strength of his squad that he did not feel it necessary to make any significant signings. It was not just Stewart who was optimistic; the fans, the players and the *South Wales Football Echo* all agreed with Stewart's stance, such had been the improvement in the team's performances in the second half of the previous season:

> At the start of the season the City's supporters appear to be justified in hoping for big things, and in taking an optimistic view of the future. In the first place they realise that the City directors are in the happy position of being able to command the services of all the players who made history last season, and thus there has been no necessity for introducing new 'class' players. The popular captain, Charlie Brittan, aptly summed up the situation the other day when he said, 'We ought to do well, seeing that the present season opens as a sort of continuation of the glorious run we had last year. The players are all fit and well, and if we do no more than reproduce our old form it must needs be a great side that will stem our progress'.

The confidence in the strength of the team was perhaps misguided, as while Cardiff initially started the season well, winning three and drawing one of their first five games, they then suffered a severe slump which saw them win only once in their next 11 games. One northern critic, who witnessed two of Cardiff's displays, felt that although the players were talented they were not working as hard as they should:

> I have seen most of the prominent clubs this season, and very few are more capable than Cardiff when the Welshmen are at their best. Their efforts, however, are too short lived, they dazzle with their brilliance one minute and then fall away so badly as to create the impression they were lacking in earnestness. They are not without skill individually and collectively, and there should be no need to worry about the future if the players more fully realised that they must be triers at all times.

Cardiff's forward line also came in for heavy criticism due to their profligacy in front of goal. It was, however, recognised that both Gill and Davies were quality players, and though some cried out for new forwards to be bought, the *South Wales Football Echo* backed the pair to rediscover their form:

> That the introduction of new blood into Cardiff City's front rank may increase the scoring ability I have no doubt, but it is not an easy matter to pick up or even secure by the payment of heavy transfer fees better qualified players than are at present on Cardiff City's list. All who have some knowledge of the control of big clubs must know full well that there would be many eager managers prepared to make big bids for the Cardiff players who might be substituted by the 'new blood' if they were put on the transfer list. The position is really a peculiar one, as it is not improbable that the introduction of a new player known to possess less football ability than the one he supplants would prove a success for a time from a goalscoring point of view.

Stewart was under increasing pressure and felt that he had no option but to make a move in the transfer market. Consequently, in December 1922, he signed George Reid, a forward from Walsall, and Fergus Aitken from Blackburn Rovers. Reid made a promising start to his Cardiff career as he scored on his debut, in a 5–1 win for the Bluebirds at Manchester City, and he then scored vital goals in wins against West Bromwich Albion and Bolton Wanderers.

Reid's introduction to the team had the desired effect, as not only did Cardiff start winning again, but it also meant that he gave much needed competition to Len Davies and Jimmy Gill, who had both been disappointing in the first half of the season.

Once Davies got his chance back in the side, due to Reid being Cup tied, he never looked back as he scored nine goals in his next six games, including a hat-trick in a 6–1 win over Chelsea. After Reid's arrival, Gill's form also dramatically improved as he scored 11 goals in eight games and also managed to score a hat-trick in a 5–0 win over Blackburn Rovers.

Cardiff now boasted three forwards all playing at their peak, and it showed as they began to blow away any opposition put before them with awesome attacking displays. Even Fred was among the goals during the team's goalscoring hot streak when, despite being renowned for having a woeful shot, he was asked to deputise in attack due to an injury crisis at the club. In the three games he played as a forward Fred managed to score three goals, including a double in a 2–2 draw with Burnley. Fred was as shocked as everybody else at his goalscoring form. He said of his time playing as a forward: 'It caused a bit of a sensation for a time, and one of the dressing room wags kept telling Jimmy Gill that he was not likely to get his place back.'

While Fred would return to his position at the heart of defence, he revealed what he thought made a successful goalscoring forward and the reason for his goals: 'How then did I get those goals? My only answer is having a shot at every opportunity. Yes, give me a player who will have a crack at goal as often as possible. It made little difference to me if he ballooned the ball into the roof of the stand as long as he had a go.'

Such was the depth and quality of Cardiff's squad during this spell that even when they lost six players due to international call-ups the team still managed to beat Sheffield United 1–0 at Bramall Lane.

The second half of the 1922–23 season had seen the Bluebirds hit a devastating patch of form. At one point the team scored an incredible 19 goals in just five games at Ninian Park. The team's early-season struggle to score goals was very much forgotten as they eventually finished as the League's top goalscorers, having scored a total of 73 goals. Cardiff had cemented their reputation as one of the most exciting teams in the country, but their poor early season form cost them, as they finished in ninth place.

In the Cup, Cardiff started slowly as it took them three games to finally beat Watford. In the next round the team faced Leicester and managed to defeat them at the first time of asking, with Len Davies scoring the game's only goal at Filbert Street.

Waiting for Cardiff in the next stage of the competition was their 'bogey' team, Tottenham Hotspur. The game at Ninian Park was played in atrocious conditions with the pitch a sea of mud, made worse by the driving wind and rain, which at times seemed to reach hurricane force.

Cardiff could not settle in the horrendous weather but Spurs rose above it and cruised into a 3–0 half-time lead. With nothing to lose, Cardiff came out fighting in the second half and Gill managed to score an early goal, which was then followed up by a Jack Evans penalty to make the score 3–2. With 20 minutes still remaining the Cardiff players put in a titanic effort, but the all-important equalising goal eluded them. With fans, players and officials all caught up in the mesmerising game Fred recalled an amusing incident concerning the Tottenham manager: 'Three minutes from the end the ball was kicked into the stand and caught by the Spurs manager. He was so completely under the spell of the game that he held the ball, at the same time indicating to his players that only a few minutes remained. The crowd shouted their protest, but, of course, Mr McWilliam did not hold up the game deliberately.'

While the Bluebirds once more lost out to Tottenham Hotspur, they did fare a little better in the Welsh Cup as they again won the trophy with a hard-fought 3–2 win against Aberdare Athletic in the Final.

CHAPTER 5

THE START OF THE GLORY YEARS

Season 1923–24

With the Bluebirds flying during the second half of the 1922–23 season, Fred Stewart again felt that he did not need to make any major additions to his squad. While he signed six players for small fees, Cardiff's first XI now boasted an arsenal of defensive and attacking talent and were recognised as a real threat.

A director of Cardiff City told the annual meeting of shareholders: 'We have much to be thankful for in being able to rely upon the services of the players who did so well last season, and I might tell you that we are envied by nearly all the other League clubs.'

The optimism in the strength of the team would this time around prove to be well founded, as the upcoming season was the most successful Cardiff City have ever had in the top flight of English football.

A change in captaincy was required at the start of the season when the former captain, Charlie Brittan, left the club having lost his place in the team to Jimmy Nelson. Cardiff were fortunate that they boasted many candidates who were able to fill Brittan's shoes, not least Jimmy Blair, the Scotland captain. After much deliberation it was decided that Blair would be appointed as Cardiff captain while Fred would act as his deputy.

As had been predicted, Cardiff started the season in fantastic form, going the first 11 games unbeaten. Cardiff forward Len Davies hit a purple patch during this period as he scored eight times. On 10 November 1923, Davies also scored all four goals in Cardiff's 4–2 win over West Bromwich Albion.

Such was Cardiff's reputation for exciting football that FA Secretary Mr J.F. Wall visited Ninian Park to watch the Bluebirds draw 1–1 with Chelsea. Cardiff missed a number of chances to win the game, but nevertheless Mr Wall was impressed by their display and following the game he informed Fred Stewart that he thought that he had built a 'great' team.

On 27 October 1923, Cardiff's fine run of form finally came to an end in spectacular style when the team imploded at Preston, conceding three goals in just 13 minutes. It would not be long, however, before Cardiff put this defeat behind them as they proceeded to beat West Brom 3–0 and 4–2 in the following two games.

Cardiff were back on track, and after a particularly impressive 3–0 win at Sunderland, a proud Fred Stewart said that the game was: 'the greatest I have ever witnessed and I have never seen our lads play such wonderful football'.

The *South Wales Football Echo* were also complimentary about the team's efforts at Sunderland: 'That Cardiff City possesses players of undoubted ability is beyond questions, but an all-important point is that they harmonise. That, in a nutshell, is the secret of their success.'

Despite being top of the League, and blowing away most teams with awesome displays of attacking and defensive strength, some fans of the team still demanded more. The *Football Echo* said of this attitude: 'I am afraid that the regular supporters – those who attend match after match at Ninian Park – are sometimes lacking in their appreciation of the team and do not always realise how fortunate they are in being provided with so many opportunities of seeing so fine a side in action.'

Cardiff's imperious displays were aided by Billy Hardy, who was in scintillating form. Many pundits proclaimed that Hardy was the best half-back in the country and should be playing for England. Regardless of this, the England selectors refused to pick him as he was playing for a Welsh club. There was much controversy regarding this decision and the *Liverpool Echo* gave this verdict: 'The present policy of the FA in depriving a Cardiff City player English international honours, however high his abilities, to our mind savours of ultra-conservatism, red-tapism, narrow-mindedness, or call it what you will, as C.B. Fry would say.'

Fred Stewart had always thought highly of Hardy and was disappointed that one of his favourite players was not getting the recognition that he deserved: 'He has never played a bad game in his life. Therefore it is not surprising that he has never been left out of the team as a matter of form. Cardiff City would rejoice if he were to be honoured by the English Association for he is a wonderful half-back.'

While the team was challenging at the top of the table Stewart was still tempted into the transfer market when he signed Scottish winger Dennis Lawson from St Mirren. This signing allowed Cardiff to sell Billy Grimshaw to Sunderland for the then massive fee of £4,000. Grimshaw had been an excellent servant to the club, having been a virtual ever present the previous four seasons, but the chance to obtain a substantial transfer fee for him proved too much for the directors to turn down.

On 15 December 1923, amid much hype, the team made their way to Anfield to play the champions, Liverpool. If there was any doubt that Cardiff were indeed the real deal then this was quickly dispelled as they comfortably beat the scousers 2–0. The *Football Echo* said of this impressive display: 'The old champions may take consolation from the fact that it was not due to faulty work on their part that they were beaten, they simply met a team that was better balanced, more capable in combination and more expert in ball control.'

Cardiff were a team playing at the top of their game, and Fred Stewart revealed how he had managed to put together such a high-quality team, with so little funds, and still get them to play like champions in the making: 'We get players of decent ability, and each man does his best, with unity of feeling and purpose. The big point is that we are all such good friends – not only the players but the directors also. We take each other's opinion. We never make a change in the team without consulting the players. Their opinion is worth having.'

Such was Cardiff's dominance during this period that from 12 October 1923 to 13 December 1923 they did not lose a single game before eventually going down at Aston Villa. Cardiff were, however, soon back on track when they beat Arsenal three times in three consecutive weeks due to playing them twice in the League and once in the Cup. On 26 January 1924, Jimmy Gill even managed to score a hat-trick against the Gunners in a 4–0 home win.

Over the course of this winning streak Fred was in majestic form as he deputised as captain while Blair was out injured. His performance as captain, against Sheffield United in particular, silenced the doubters who still tried to claim that Fred was no more than a glorified thug: 'What impressed me most was the remarkable vitality of Keenor. He is something more than a mere grafter. All his efforts indicated the possession in a high degree of football intelligence. He would open up the play by swinging out to the wings, or vary his methods by initiating close passing, but there was always an object in view. And what a great goal did he score. It was the work of a strategist to spring a surprise on opponents in that way and effect so neat a combination with Lawson before cutting in and scoring.'

It was not just his intelligence in reading the game and distributing the ball that caught the eye, it was also his wholehearted effort and determination. Fred Stewart said of him: 'Fred Keenor sums up the attitude of our team. I honestly do not believe the word "beaten" is in his vocabulary.'

One reporter wrote: 'Seeing him in action, you would think that the be-all and end-all of his life was football.'

With just two months of the season remaining, Cardiff sat at the top of the table and looked to be marching towards the First Division title. Huddersfield and Sunderland were the only teams that had any hope of catching the trailblazing Cardiff juggernaut.

But then, out of nowhere, the wheels suddenly came off in spectacular fashion. From 16 February 1924 to 7 April 1924 Cardiff failed to win a single game. During this spell they also lost 2–0 to their title rivals Huddersfield, managed by legendary manager Herbert Chapman, and lost twice to mid-table Notts County. There were mitigating circumstances for the home Notts

County defeat, however, as five of Cardiff's players were away on international duty at the time. This was before the days when games would be postponed if there were Welsh international games, and Cardiff therefore duly paid the price for having a successful team full of international players.

A Cardiff match programme said of this predicament: 'This season will probably be remembered for our bid for the Championship of the League, a task which has been rendered doubly difficult owing to the demands made on the club for players to take part in international contests. It will be no surprise if the few points lost through being compelled to field weaker teams may prove to be our undoing.'

The *Football Echo*, with an air of paranoia pervading one of its articles, felt that many teams were increasing their efforts against Cardiff as they did not want a Welsh side to win the League: 'Their experience is that the English teams do not relish the possibility of an English League Championship going to a Welsh club, and in order to stem the latter's progress they are more concerned with the task of preventing Cardiff City from getting into their stride than of making the games a test of football ability.'

Another contributing factor in this winless phase was the loss of key players Herbie Evans and Len Davies due to injury. When Davies eventually returned to the team the Bluebirds marched back to the top of the table, going through April unbeaten and dropping just two points out of a maximum of 14 on offer. At this stage teams were still being awarded only two points for a win.

As Cardiff went into the final League game of the season, away to Birmingham City, they were still top of the League and only a catastrophic series of results that day could prevent them becoming First Division League champions for the first time in their history. All Cardiff had to do was win at Birmingham and the title would be theirs.

If Cardiff did not win, however, then Huddersfield would need to win their game by three clear goals. The Terriers were playing lowly Nottingham Forest at home, but had only managed to scrape a draw against them in the previous game. Many critics therefore thought that Huddersfield beating Forest by three clear goals was unlikely, particularly as Huddersfield were not renowned for their goalscoring prowess; however, Forest had struggled all season and going into the last game they had nothing left to play for, so it was not beyond the bounds of possibility that Huddersfield could still do it if Cardiff failed to win.

Despite the odds weighing heavily in Cardiff's favour, the team still somehow managed to throw away the title in heartbreaking fashion on a day of unprecedented drama. With a little over 20 minutes remaining at St Andrew's, and the game still scoreless, Cardiff City were awarded a penalty, after Jimmy Gill's goal-bound header was handballed on the goalline by a Birmingham defender. Len Davies, the prolific Cardiff forward, stepped up to take the penalty, knowing that a goal would probably result in Cardiff winning the title. The pressure obviously took its toll on Davies, as his tame kick went straight at the Birmingham 'keeper.

At Huddersfield, the score was 1–0 with less than 20 minutes to go. If the score remained the same Cardiff would be champions, regardless of Davies's penalty miss.

Unbelievably, in those final 20 minutes Huddersfield scored a further two goals to win the game 3–0, and with it capture the first of three consecutive Championships. This meant that Cardiff let the League title slip from their grasp by a goal average difference of just 0.024. No other team in history has ever missed out on the League title by such a small margin.

In later years, Fred said of Len Davies's penalty miss at Birmingham: 'There is no doubt that the excitement and the knowledge that so much depended on the shot unnerved Len a little. Under ordinary circumstances it would have been a gift goal, but Len Davies muffed the kick and the ball rolled gently to the goalkeeper, who calmly gathered and made an easy clearance.'

Despite the crushing disappointment of missing out on the title by the slenderest of margins, the Cardiff fans still came out in force to give their side a hero's welcome when they arrived back from Birmingham at Cardiff Central train station.

The League season may have ended on a sour note, but Cardiff had enjoyed another encouraging FA Cup run when the team had again reached the quarter-final stage of the competition. Unfortunately, the team progressed no further as they lost 1–0 to Manchester City in a replay. It was Fred's former Wales teammate Billy Meredith who, at 50 years of age, produced a moment of magic to set up the winning goal in extra-time. Fred said that Meredith had hardly touched the ball, but when it mattered he had produced the telling moment that had won the game.

Over the course of the season the team once again won many plaudits for their exciting style of play and their conduct on the pitch. A referee, who had officiated over some of Cardiff's matches during the season, was so impressed with the team's attitude that he wrote to the club and said: 'I must say you have got together a most gentlemanly lot of players who never quibble over decisions, although, perhaps, there may have been some they did not agree with, but they took them smiling, and I do sincerely trust it may fall to my lot to have charge of your team on many occasions, when I feel sure they will always endeavour to play the game as clean in future games as they have done in the two games I have just had.'

Fred had epitomised the team's respectful approach towards officials, not only over the course of the season, but also throughout his career. In 1937 he even wrote an article defending referees entitled 'Knights of the Whistle' and said: 'I do not want to pose as a lecturer, but, as an old player, I am emphatic in my view that the referee is very often wrongly blamed. Of course, I could quote instances where I think the referee has been in the wrong, but in my playing days they were not a bad lot.'

Not only was the season memorable for Fred, due to Cardiff's challenge for the title, but it was also another noteworthy year for his international career. On 16 February 1924, Fred captained Wales when they took on Scotland at Ninian Park. In a proud day for Cardiff City, Jimmy Blair also captained Scotland, so for the first and only time in the club's history two of their players captained their national sides, playing against each other. It was only proper that this should happen at Ninian Park. The two captains also played the game wearing Cardiff's club shorts and socks, as in those days international players were expected to supply these items themselves. To complete a perfect day for Fred, Wales went on to win the game 2–0, which gave Fred bragging rights as he and Blair walked home together after the match.

Two weeks after the Scotland game Fred again captained Wales as they took on the old enemy, England, at Blackburn. Fred's performance that day was described as 'brilliant' as he set up the first goal following a 'scintillating run, beating four opponents and smashing a magnificent drive which Sewell in the English goal could only parry'. Wales, spurred on by Fred dominating proceedings, went on to win the game 2–0.

For just the second time in their history Wales won the Victory Championship when they beat Ireland in Belfast. Despite just missing out on the title with Cardiff City, Fred did at least have the consolation of winning silverware for his country of which he was very proud.

In May 1924, Cardiff City embarked on their first overseas tour when they visited Czechoslovakia, Austria and Germany. The team travelled for three days by train and the cross-channel ferry in order to reach Czechoslovakia, where they would take on Sparta Prague in a friendly game. The game was anything but a friendly, however, as the Prague players pulled, pushed and kicked the Cardiff players off the ball. At the interval a furious Fred was so disgusted at Prague's foul play that as he walked off the pitch he uttered a terrifying promise to the Prague players: 'If I get many more kicks on the shin I shall be chopping someone off at the knees.'

As the team came out for the second half the crowd had grown increasingly hostile, and with police protection being minimal many Cardiff City players received kicks and punches from spectators when they took throw-ins and corner-kicks. In the end Cardiff lost the game 3–2, but the players were just glad to leave the intimidating stadium all in one piece.

Following the mayhem in Prague the team then travelled to Austria, where they faced First Vienna. Cardiff beat the Austrian side 2–0, but Fred, ever the football enthusiast, was particularly impressed with their continental style of football. He said: 'The short passing of the Austrians was really amazing and most of it was done with the toe and not the instep.'

After the victory over Vienna the team then travelled to Germany where they beat Borussia Dortmund 2–0 and drew 2–2 with SV Hamburg. Fred was impressed with the German style of football, which he felt was a direct style of a 'high standard'.

Fred and the team had enjoyed their first foreign football adventure as they had learnt new styles of play from their opponents, which they were keen to implement back home. The food on offer was the only complaint from their travels and the players were glad to return to England so that they could enjoy a good British meal. Fred said: 'The first thing we asked for on reaching London was a big steak and chips.'

To top off a successful season for club and country, Muriel Keenor gave birth to the family's third child, Alfred.

Season 1924–25

Over the course of the previous year Fred had set about building his young family a home in the relatively affluent Cardiff suburb of Whitchurch. Unlike the superstars of today he did not hire a famous architect to design it, nor did he sit back while a team of builders built it: Fred designed and helped build the house himself.

When designing the house Fred was adamant that it should have a big garden, so that he could continue his hobby of flower growing. Fred's favourite flowers were dahlias and he would say that nothing would annoy him more than when frost would play havoc with his blooms. He also claimed that gardening was one of the best methods for keeping fit: 'An hour's digging is as good as an hour's punch-ball'.

As well as growing flowers in the garden, Fred also spent lots of his spare time in an allotment, just 200 yards from his house, where he would grow vegetables.

Fred's competitive spirit was so fervent that many felt that one of the reasons he spent so much care and time growing his vegetables and flowers was because he secretly wanted them to win prizes in order to show that he did know something other than football. In reality it seems that whatever Fred did, whether football or gardening, he wanted to be the best and could not settle for doing something to merely enjoy it.

Dogs were also one of Fred's passions, and at this time he bought a young Irish Terrier for him and his young family to enjoy. Yet Fred was not happy with any old family dog; he had to have the best dog. He would subsequently be seen at local dog shows with his Irish Terrier attempting to win a prize for best of breed. It is hard to imagine international footballers taking their pets to a dog show today.

Another of Fred's favourite pastimes, which he enjoyed with his family, was 'motoring'. His favourite touring ground was North Wales, where he enjoyed the spectacular scenery, but on occasion these motoring trips did not always go to plan, as he revealed in an interview:

> I was taking the wife and youngsters to Aberystwyth and we had been all day on the road. At about ten o'clock at night, the car developed magneto trouble. We were about six miles from our destination, and I tried a road-side repair. I was unlucky, however, so I stopped a passing motorist, and asked him to take a message to the nearest garage with a view to getting a tow home.
>
> We waited hour after hour. The wife and children went to sleep in the car, while I waited for the expected assistance. It did not come, however, and at five o'clock I commenced the long trudge for help. When we eventually got into the town we all went straight to bed, after baths and breakfast, and slept soundly for the rest of the day.

Fred's love of his car was also the source of a lot of practical jokes played on him by his Cardiff City teammates. After training, other players who owned cars would purposely block Fred's car in so that he could not leave. Much to the amusement of Fred's teammates, he would turn the air blue with expletives until one of them finally moved their car.

Music was also an obsession in the Keenor household as Muriel was an accomplished pianist. At least twice a week Fred and his family would gather around the piano and sing popular songs of the day.

One thing was for sure: the boy from humble surroundings in Roath had now blossomed into a family man with a house that was totally different from the cramped home that he grew up in. Yet Fred remained at heart a working-class man and did not forget his roots.

With his family settled into their new abode, Fred's focus turned to the forthcoming 1924–25 season. It would be hard to improve on the success of the previous season, but the forthcoming year would again prove to be memorable.

Fred Stewart refused to rest on his laurels and was busy in the transfer market during the off-season, signing no fewer than 10 players. One of his signings, Harold Beadles, had been at Cardiff on trial just after the war, but Stewart had neglected to sign him on that occasion. Another of Stewart's acquisitions, Willie Davies, had helped keep Cardiff's bitter rivals, Swansea Town, in business after Cardiff paid the sum of £2,500 for the player, which helped Swansea avoid going into liquidation.

In one of the most remarkable signings that Cardiff City has ever made, Fred Stewart also signed a deaf and dumb player by the name of James McLean from Barn Athletic. Unfortunately, McLean did not make any first-team appearances for the Bluebirds and he was subsequently released at the end of the season.

After the success of the previous season there was record interest in tickets to watch Cardiff City play. A match programme said: 'Every seat in the Canton and Grange Inner Stands have been allotted while but a few remain in the Centre Stand. If the whole of the tickets are taken up, it will probably prove a boon to the holders, as it may be possible then to grant Season Ticket holders the privilege they have been urgently demanding of admittance to Cup-tie matches in preference to others.'

There has often been an accusation levelled at Cardiff City that when there is a high level of interest in the club they invariably let you down – and this season was to be no exception. Cardiff won just once in their opening five games and looked a shadow of the team that had come so close to being champions just a few short months previously. Performances did pick up eventually, but consistency was a major problem.

THE START OF THE GLORY YEARS

Again, the number of internationals the club had on its books did not always help matters as it had regularly to do without them when they were called-up for international duty. On one memorable occasion, however, when seven first-team players were away playing for Wales, Scotland and Ireland, Cardiff still managed to beat Newcastle United 3–0.

After missing the vital penalty at the end of the previous season against Birmingham City, Len Davies recovered to enjoy another productive season in front of goal, where he finished as the team's top goalscorer with 20 goals in 30 games.

Fred, along with Davies, was one of the few players to continue his good form from the previous season. Of one game against Newcastle, in which he wore the captain's armband due to Blair being injured, the *Football Echo* wrote: 'Keenor was entrusted with the captaincy, and he covered himself with glory. His enthusiasm was contagious; he brought out the best in his colleagues, and if there was one department more than another in which the City had a big advantage over Newcastle it was at half-back, for the flank men came up to Keenor's standard.'

The team's League form may have been disappointing, as they eventually finished in 11th place, but the same could not be said of their Cup form. Cardiff had started the competition slowly, taking three attempts to beat lowly Darlington, much to the disgust of the Cardiff fans, who booed the team off the field.

In light of the crowd's reaction to the team during the Darlington game, the match programme for the second-round clash with Fulham pleaded for tolerance: 'A few cheers for our lads will not be out of place (the most surprised will be the players). Don't boo the referee. He'll be doing his best. Angels can do no more.'

The comments again show that while some things have changed in the game, fans will always become frustrated when they feel their team is underperforming, and they will barrack a referee if they believe that he has made a bad decision.

Cardiff were once again unconvincing in the second round of the Cup when, in monsoon-like conditions, they struggled to a 1–0 win over the Londoners

85

at Ninian Park. The conditions were so horrendous that at one point the rain was coming down so hard that the game had to be suspended for 10 minutes before play could resume.

The weather would no doubt have hampered the players' performances, as not only would they all have been wearing heavy boots, but their kits would also have been made from thick cotton, which would soak up the rain. This, coupled with the fact that pitches were poorly kept, and the balls were like rocks to kick in wet weather, contributed to the Cardiff players struggling to play attractive football in such testing conditions.

The team finally started to hit top gear in the next round when, despite not having Len Davies in the team due to injury, they beat Notts County 2–0 at Meadow Lane. Jimmy Gill scored a fantastic second goal which was described in Cardiff City's next home match programme: 'The goal by Gill was the finest exhibition of artistry ever seen. With the ball at his feet, he eluded opponent after opponent, all after him like terriers, and when he placed the ball in the net he gave Iremonger no chance.'

This result meant that Cardiff had again reached the quarter-finals of the Cup for the fourth consecutive season. The Cardiff fans had been frustrated at the team's progress in the FA Cup in previous years, as they always seemed to get so close to reaching the Final, only to blow it. On this occasion Cardiff would have to defeat Leicester City to progress any further in the competition, and there was a real belief that this could be the year when they would finally reach Wembley.

The fanfare before the game was well justified, as a crowd of 50,272 would witness one of the most dramatic games ever seen at Ninian Park. Beadles had given Cardiff an early lead, but Leicester hit back with an equaliser from Duncan. What followed was a sensational end-to-end game, with both sides having chances to score, before Willie Davies scored the most improbable winner, direct from a corner, with the last kick of the game.

The referee blew the final whistle as soon as the ball had entered the net but the players and spectators were not sure whether the goal had stood. This had been the first season in which a player had been allowed to score a goal direct from a corner-kick and many of the fans, and even some of the players, were unaware of the rule change. Willie Davies said of his goal: 'I took it in a hurry with my right foot. The swerve on the ball beat everybody and it went into the net. I had forgotten, in the excitement, that a goal could now be scored direct from the corner flag, but the next minute I was being mobbed by thousands of spectators.'

Fred recalled the pandemonium that broke out after the final whistle: 'Immediately after the ball had entered the net the whistle went, and the crowd, in their confusion, invaded the field in their thousands. They did not know whether the City had won or not. It seemed that I was asked a million times whether the goal had counted, but, frankly, I was not certain myself. After a hectic struggle through the excited crowd I reached the dressing room and the first man to whom I dashed was the referee. I asked him if it was a goal. "Of course it was," he replied, "but there was no time to restart the game."'

When the fans were finally informed by Jimmy Blair that the goal had stood there was absolute bedlam as celebrations broke out throughout the stadium. The *Football Echo* described the ecstatic scenes after it was confirmed that Cardiff had won the game: 'The crowd swarmed on the pitch to congratulate the players. They crowded in front of the stand, and it was with difficulty that the police kept them from rushing the barriers to reach the dressing room, with a view of showing their appreciation of Willie Davies. A scene of this nature I have never witnessed.'

The Bluebirds were drawn against formidable opposition in the semi-finals; five times Cup-winners Blackburn Rovers. At the time both teams were rooted in mid-table and a tight game was therefore predicted.

The match that followed at Meadow Lane was certainly not in the script as Cardiff shot into an unassailable three-goal lead in the opening 20 minutes. Blackburn pulled one goal back, but Cardiff went on to win the game and were through to their first-ever FA Cup Final. Fred was in majestic form that day and the *Daily Mirror* said of his display: 'Keenor literally had Puddefoot in his pocket...the only Blackburn man to come out of the game with an enhanced reputation was Healless. His was a sound display all through, though he was not nearly so dominant as Keenor.'

Fred felt that the Cardiff team were a force to be reckoned with and that the players deserved their day at Wembley as a reward for their incredible efforts: 'The truth is that on the form we showed during that opening quarter of an hour we would have licked any team in the world...I think we deserve it. We are 11 triers, and all are real triers.'

The Cardiff match programme, reporting on the semi-final victory, was equally full of praise for Fred Stewart's men: 'Never shall I forget the almost magical scoring which took place at Meadow Lane. Three goals in 17 minutes and that in a semi-final! It was a match won by a brilliant side through skill and determination, and those of us who had the privilege of witnessing it will ever remember the loyalty of the men who wrought, who gave of their best for the club and the town of their adoption and who gained by their efforts imperishable fame.'

News of Cardiff's famous victory delighted City fans all over the globe. The *Football Echo* published a letter that it had received from Cardiff fans living in the USA: 'Early this week I received an interesting letter dated March 20, from some Welsh boys at Scranton, USA, extending their congratulations to the City upon their Cup-tie successes. The writer recalls the old Southern League days when he was a regular supporter of the City, and he has not failed to follow the club's career since leaving these shores for America. "Our shouts of 'Play up the City' cannot be heard," he writes, "but my friends and I wish the team the best of luck, and we hope they will bring the Cup to Cardiff."'

Cardiff would meet fearsome opposition in the Final; four times FA Cup-winners Sheffield United. With most football fans in South Wales desperate to see the game the FA had drastically underestimated the insatiable demand for tickets and had unbelievably allocated only 1,750 tickets out of a possible 92,000 to Cardiff City fans. After lodging a protest Cardiff eventually managed to obtain 4,000 tickets, but this was still not enough to satisfy the masses. Despite the shortage of tickets, 40,000 Cardiff fans still somehow managed to see their team play at Wembley. It goes to show that it is not just in today's game that tickets at big matches get taken up by 'the prawn sandwich brigade' ahead of loyal supporters.

Unfortunately, despite the pre-match hype, the Final turned out to be an anti-climax with both teams struggling to reach top form. Cardiff in particular did not play to their potential as they missed their talismanic striker Len Davies, who was absent due to injury. Years later it was also revealed just how nervous the Cardiff players were prior to the Final when Billy Hardy said: 'We went out shaking like kittens.'

As is so often the way in high-profile games, the match was decided by an error. In the 30th minute the Cardiff right-half, Harry Wake, was caught in possession on the edge of the penalty area by the England international, Fred Tunstall. Tunstall bore down on goal and dispatched the ball beyond Farquharson into the net. Fred, as ever the leader, would absolve Wake of any blame when describing the goal in an interview: 'Harry Wake was in possession of the ball and was facing his own goal when he turned to make a clearance. Tunstall, sizing up the position much quicker than any of our defence, raced in, robbed Wake on the turn, and after advancing about 10 yards shot into the far corner of the net. Any blame must be shouldered by the rest of the defence of which I was one. A warning shout should have been given of Tunstall's first approach. Wake could not have been aware of it, but credit must be given to Tunstall for using his brains and feet so quickly. Tunstall was a great footballer in his day, and was a real match-winner if ever there was one.'

The solitary goal was enough for Sheffield United as they went on to win the game and seemingly shatter the Bluebirds' dreams of becoming the first team from outside England to win the FA Cup. Cardiff may have lost the game, but Fred had delivered another all-action performance. The *Daily Mirror* said: 'Fred Keenor, the Welsh international centre-half, was the dominating personality of the game...Keenor was Cardiff's biggest match-winning asset'.

While being disappointed in the manner of the defeat, Fred, in his usual tub-thumping way, said: 'Just because we lost in our very first Cup Final, I don't think there is any cause to get down in the mouth. I can say here and now that one day soon our followers can be sure that Cardiff City will bring that cup to Wales.'

Yet in a later interview Fred would reveal his hurt and frustration at not winning the Cup when he said about his FA Cup-runners'-up medal: 'It should have been a winner's but we won't go over all that again.'

Following the end of the season the team went on a tour of Ireland where they played and beat Bohemians 7–1. The president of the Irish club was Major-General Emmett Dalton, who had been right-hand man to Michael Collins, the leader of the IRA, during the troubles of 1919–21. At one point Dalton had been one of the British Government's most wanted men, but following Cardiff's match against Bohemians he followed the team's results and stayed in touch with the club for many years.

Season 1925–26

Even though the team had not been successful in winning a trophy, Cardiff City had reached extraordinary heights in the previous two seasons, having just missed out on the First Division title and the FA Cup. The Cardiff team was determined that the 1925–26 season would be the one in which they finally brought some trophies to Ninian Park. The Cardiff fans were also confident that this would be their year, as the *Football Echo* emphasised: 'Supporters of Cardiff City are justified in believing that the team will do well this season. All the players who contributed to the success of the club last year are again available, and thus no time need be spent in settling down. The players know each other's styles to perfection, and in this respect they have the advantage over other clubs that have been compelled to introduce new talent.'

However, a momentous change in the laws of the game was announced before the season got underway, concerning the offside rule. It was decided that in the forthcoming season a player would not be offside if two, instead of three, opponents were in front of him when the ball was played forwards for that player to receive. The change had been made to encourage more goals, as there was obviously more chance of a forward scoring a goal if he only had to worry about getting past two opposing players in front of him instead of three. Indeed, the new rule appeared to have the desired effect, with Middlesbrough's George Camsell scoring a record 59 goals in the 1926–27 season. Dixie Dean, the famous Everton forward, would of course famously go on to beat that record the following season when he scored 60 goals, a record that has never been surpassed.

Dean was one of English football's superstars at this time, and during a Wales versus England international game, Fred had targeted him as England's dangerman. Subsequently Fred spent the first-half intimidating Dean verbally and physically in an attempt to put him off his game. As the sides walked off the pitch at half-time Fred then allegedly called him a 'black-headed bastard'. This was a step too far, as Dean snapped:

> I caught him at half-time under the gangway as we were going into the dressing rooms. Somebody pulled my right hand back. Otherwise one of us would have been taken to hospital and the other one – me – would have been sent off…It was a policeman who'd got hold of me but when the authorities knew the full strength of what Keenor had said to me I was let off and Keenor had to write an apology, which he did and that was that.
>
> That fella would kick his own mother for a couple of bob. All he could do was kick or try to cripple somebody. He'd set himself out to do it.

However, a future teammate of Fred's, Ernie Curtis, would argue that he was not a dirty player, just a hard one:

> He was one of the hardest tacklers in the game. Some said he was dirty but he was just hard. He could run all night, he couldn't run with the ball mind you, but he could run all day. Nobody took liberties with old Fred. I would have liked to have seen him against today's fancy dans with their elbowing, shirt-pulling and poking out tongues. Fred would have tackled them once – they wouldn't come back for more.

Ernie Curtis would also reveal just how Fred was able to 'run all day' as he built up his incredible stamina with an unorthodox training regime: 'He was fit considering he was a chain smoker. He would lap Ninian Park in a pair of old heavy army boots while we were doing ball practice.'

It was said that Fred was famously partial to a drink and would regularly turn up to training late, ignore his teammates and trainers, and begin running laps around the Ninian Park pitch in order to work off the excess of the previous night. It was an approach that obviously worked for him, as he was one of the fittest players in the Cardiff City team. There can be little doubt that this preparation for top-class football would most certainly be frowned upon by current managers such as Arsène Wenger and Sir Alex Ferguson!

With the new offside rule in place the players and management at Cardiff were concerned as to how the team would adapt. Therefore before the season started Cardiff played a trial game that incorporated the new rule. A reporter from the *Football Echo* watched the game:

> In the trial game played at Ninian Park the spectators were delighted to find that the first-team forwards were prompt in making the most of the opportunities that came their way through the changed formation in the opposing defence, and this gave rise to increased optimism with regard to the future, but sight must not be lost of the fact that other teams are possessed of clever forwards, and it may happen that while the City may figure more prominently as goalscorers, opposing teams may also develop a talent in that direction and heavy scoring will be the order.
>
> We must hold ourselves in patience for a time, as I have previously intimated, before claiming for Cardiff City an advantage over other clubs through the alteration in the rule. Certain it is that less will be seen of the disappointing stoppages when the forwards moved along in perfect harmony occasioned by one of the two defending backs taking a step forward in anticipation of a pass. It is all very well for some to say that an intelligent set of forwards should always succeed against the old defensive methods, but the fact remains that in many games the attack was crippled and the spectators became disgruntled because of

the incessant free-kicks. In that part the City appear to have been chief sufferers, and to their credit, be it said, they have not made a practice of indulging in the style of play.

It was obvious from watching the trial match that Cardiff could take some time to find their form until they learnt the best tactics by which to utilise the new rule.

In light of this it was unsurprising that Cardiff got off to a slow start once the season got underway as they crashed to a 3–2 opening day defeat away to Manchester City. The game was also notable for Jimmy Nelson becoming the first Cardiff player ever to be sent off when he was involved in 'fisticuffs' with a member of the Manchester City team. The incident was exacerbated as it occurred in the Cardiff penalty area, in the last minute of the game, when the score was tied at 2–2. Nelson was dismissed and Manchester City scored the winning goal from the penalty spot. Nelson was banned for four weeks and subsequently missed seven matches owing to this misdemeanour.

After the opening-day defeat, Cardiff won only three of their next 12 games, with the team coming in for criticism following their failure to adapt to the new offside rule. The *Football Echo* said of this situation: 'The new rule is proving a source of worry. Many players experience difficulty in settling down under the new conditions, and it will be necessary for them to engage in several matches before they can be seen at their best. That there are advantages to be gained as a result of this rule is patent to all; it is reflected in the heavy scoring. Yet there are players who forget what is required of them under the new conditions, and adhere to the old methods.'

Despite his high standing with the Cardiff fans, Fred was not immune from criticism at this time. As he struggled to come to terms with the new rule he stopped his foraging runs forward, for which he was famous, and some critics felt that he had become half the player that he used to be as a by-product of this.

Keenor sometimes ran himself out through sheer love of work. The Welsh international captain is working so hard this season that in most matches he has been the outstanding figure, and quite possibly, if he refrained from dropping back to assist his colleagues behind, he would have more time to devote to constructive work, but the team would then be weaker in defence.

Fred later revealed in an interview just how hard he had found it to change his game after the new rule was implemented:

> Positional play had to be adjusted to meet the new rule, and the centre-half became a glorified full-back. He could not keep in close touch with his own attack unless he created a big gap for the opposing centre-forward.
>
> I must confess that for a time I was affected by the change. It increased the responsibility of the centre-half and shortened his playing career. It was almost impossible for him to share his duties between defence and attack. There was no happy medium, and the man who tried it did more running about than any player on the field.

It was not just Fred, and the Cardiff defence, who were being lambasted for their failure to adapt to the new rule, as the forwards were suffering from a crisis in confidence as well. After a loss to West Ham the *Football Echo* said: 'Although the City forwards did not do justice to their reputation against West Ham I am convinced they will ere long be seen to better advantage as a thrustful, aggressive side. At present they do not appear to have a fixed plan of campaign and they are not able in the circumstances to make profitable use of the advantages that should be theirs as a result of the alteration in the offside rule.'

Fred Stewart was obviously not convinced that the forwards he had at his disposal could change their game to adapt to the new rule and therefore he decided that he needed to take drastic action. He firstly made the surprise move of selling Jimmy Gill to Blackpool for the sum of £3,200. Gill had given the club five excellent seasons of service and the opportunity to sell him for such a large sum, after Cardiff had bought him for only £750, represented good business, particularly in light of his poor form following the rule change.

With Stewart allowed to use all of the proceeds from Gill's sale on player purchases, and with the directors providing him with further funds, he had a significant war chest with which to purchase new forwards. What followed was an unprecedented spending spree, which took everyone by surprise. First to come in was inside-forward Joe Cassidy from Bolton Wanderers for a fee of £3,800. The club then spent a club record sum of £5,000 on Motherwell forward Hughie Ferguson and a further £2,000 on Clyde's left-winger, George McLachlan.

The signing of Ferguson in particular was seen as a real coup, and the *Football Echo* excitedly heralded the arrival of the star player to Ninian Park:

In football circles it was regarded as a triumph for Mr Fred Stewart, the City's secretary-manager, who was responsible for prevailing upon the Scottish officials to part with their star player. Naturally, the directors are entitled to a big share of the credit, and in paying so big a transfer fee they have made it abundantly clear that they are determined to do all in their power to maintain first-class football and a First League team in Cardiff. The new player has been an outstanding forward in Scotland since the days when he, as a promising junior, was 'discovered' and introduced into the Motherwell team. He has 280 goals to his credit, but the pleasing feature is his retention of form and scoring power.

The new signings made an instant impact as they all made their debuts in a 5–2 win over Leicester City at Ninian Park. Hughie Ferguson grabbed a debut goal, but Joe Cassidy stole the show with a hat-trick. With the new signings in the side the team began to pull away from the relegation zone with a series of wins.

Unfortunately, this run of good form soon came to a dramatic end when the Bluebirds lost 3–0 to West Bromwich Albion and then followed that result up with a record 11–2 defeat to Sheffield United at Bramall Lane.

The embarrassing defeat sparked the team into action and they went on to lose just once in the next nine games. Fred dramatically found his feet during this spell as he finally came to terms with the new offside rule. The turning point for Fred seems to have come in a 2–0 win over Aston Villa where it was said:

> An improvement in the half-back line did much towards enabling the City to pick up full points against Aston Villa. Local enthusiasts were delighted, and they were more or less convinced that Keenor is just about to come into his own at centre-half. He has been a long time off his game, and there was some justification for the belief that he could not adapt himself to the altered style in play resulting upon the changed offside rules. In the early part of the season, although he tried hard, he was not an effective force in attack. Then came a long spell with just an occasional match sandwiched in between periods of idleness due to injuries, and, really, he has been handicapped as no other player has been. Moreover, his was a difficult position to adequately fill, and in being judged by his great form of last season Keenor suffered in more than one direction. All this now seems to have come to an end, and there is no one more pleased than is Keenor himself at the improvement.

With Fred back to his imperious best Cardiff won a vital game at fellow strugglers Notts County to finally ensure that the team would be safe from relegation. Cardiff had won the game 4–2, with Fred himself getting on the score sheet and Hughie Ferguson justifying his transfer fee by scoring a hat-trick. Since signing for the club Ferguson had scored an incredible 19 goals in 26 games, and without him Cardiff would probably have been relegated.

Cardiff's below-par season continued in the Cup competitions as they were knocked out of the FA Cup at the quarter-final stage by Newcastle United and were then humbled in the Welsh Cup by Third Division South side Merthyr Tydfil.

I July 1916, Fred Keenor (third down from top) in the trenches preparing to go over the top.

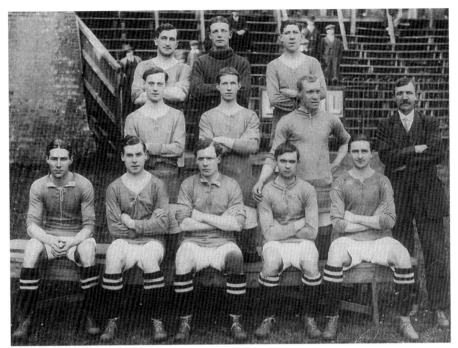

Cardiff City Reserves, South Western League, 1914–15. Fred Keenor is on the right of the back row.

Final public practice match at Ninian Park, Blues v Whites, 23 August 1919. Fred Keenor is to the left of the picture wearing a suit.

FA Cup quarter-final, 5 March 1921, Cardiff City 1 Chelsea 0. Spectators are on the girders of the partially-built Canton Stand at Ninian Park.

Old Trafford, FA Cup semi-final replay, Wolves 3 Cardiff City 1, 23 March 1921. Fred Keenor is third from the left.

Len Davies, Fred Keenor and Albert Barnett walk down Llandaff Road, Cardiff, August 1921.

Ninian Park, Wales 0 England 0, 14 March 1921.

Fred Keenor in action against Spurs during the FA Cup quarter-final replay in March 1922 at White Hart Lane.

The two Cardiff City players, Jimmy Blair of Scotland and Fred Keenor of Wales, captain their countries in an international at Ninian Park, 16 February 1924. Note both players are wearing Cardiff City shorts and socks.

St Andrew's, 13 September 1924, Birmingham City 1 Cardiff City 2. Fred Keenor is on the front row, third from the right.

Prague, 7 May 1924. The Cardiff City team defeated 3–2 by Sparta Prague. Fred Keenor is on the front row, second from the right.

Jack Evans, Joe Nicholson and Fred Keenor keeping fit at Ninian Park shortly before the 1925 Cup Final, 21 April 1925.

Fred Keenor and Sam Irving at Ninian Park in 1926–27.

FA Cup semi-final at Molineux, 26 March 1927, att: 39,476. Cardiff City 3 Reading 0. Keenor and Eggo shake hands prior to the game.

The Cardiff City 1927 FA Cup-winning team fool around in Fred Keenor's car prior to leaving for Southport. Fred Keenor is second from the right.

Muriel Keenor, Fred Keenor and a baby who is probably Gladys Keenor.

The Cardiff City team unwind at Southport Public Baths prior to the FA Cup Final, 20 April 1927. Fred Keenor is third from the right.

Friday 22 April 1927. Fred Keenor arrives in London for the FA Cup Final with Trixie the cat.

Fred Keenor introduces George McLachlan to
King George V prior to the 1927 Cup Final.

Fred Keenor clears the ball away from Arsenal's Jimmy Brain during the 1927 FA Cup Final.

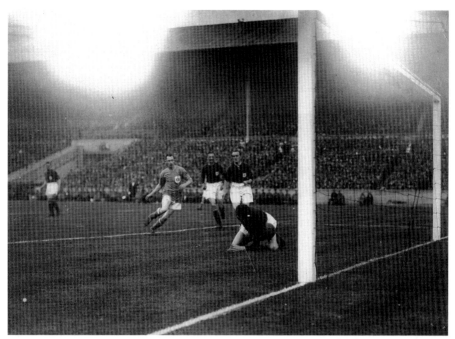

The infamous winning 1927 Cup Final goal. Arsenal goalkeeper Dan Lewis spills Hughie Ferguson's shot in to the goal.

1927 FA Cup-winning team. Top to bottom, left to right: Farquharson, Nelson, Watson, Keenor (captain), Sloan, Hardy, Curtis, Irving, Ferguson, Irving, Davies, McLachlan.

Fred Keenor, Billy Hardy and Tom Sloan walk down the Wembley steps after receiving the FA Cup from King George V.

Fred Keenor receives the crowd's applause after lifting the FA Cup.

Fred Keenor and teammates pose for photographs in the Wembley dressing room after winning the FA Cup in 1927.

Fred Keenor is escorted to the team coach while carrying the FA Cup after defeating Arsenal at Wembley in 1927.

Outside Cardiff General Station on Cardiff City's return from Wembley with the FA Cup, Monday 25 April 1927. Fred Keenor with the Cup, club chairman Walter Parker seated.

Fred Keenor with the FA Cup.

The 1927 Cardiff City FA Cup-winning team.

Fred Keenor holds his son, Brinley, in the FA Cup.

Fred Keenor captains the Welsh team to a 2–4 defeat to Scotland in 1927 at Ninian Park.

The Cardiff City 1927 FA Cup Final team with club directors. Fred Keenor is in the centre of the front row.

Penydarren Park, Merthyr, 29 April 1927. Friendly match, Merthyr Tydfil 1 Cardiff City 0, att: 8,000. Played six days after Cardiff City's FA Cup Final win at Wembley.

Scottish Cup-winners Celtic defeat FA Cup-winners Cardiff 4–1 at Hampden Park, 3 October 1927. Fred Keenor is on the front row, fourth from the left.

Cardiff City crown the opening of the new Grange End Stand at Ninian Park with a record 7–0 win over Burnley, with Hughie Ferguson scoring five, 1 September 1928. Fred Keenor is in the centre of the front row, with the ball between his knees.

Cardiff City team and directors with the FA Cup, Charity Shield and the Welsh Cup, October 1927. Fred Keenor is on the front row, third from the left.

Ninian Park, 4 January 1969, FA Cup third round, Cardiff City 0 Arsenal 0. Fred Keenor and Bob John (ex-Arsenal) discuss the 1927 Cup Final.

Following the success of the previous two seasons, the 1925–26 season was ultimately a bitter disappointment. The failure of the squad to challenge for a trophy was surprising, as between 24 October 1925 and 20 November 1925 there was a record number of 16 internationals on Cardiff's books. Harold Beadles, Len Davies, Willie Davies, Herbie Evans, Jack Evans, Fred Keenor, Jack Lewis, Jack Nicholls and Edgar Thomas were all Welsh internationals. The Scottish internationals at the club were Jimmy Blair, Joe Cassidy, Dennis Lawson and Jimmy Nelson, while the players who had represented Ireland were Tom Farquharson, Pat McIllvenny and Tommy Sloan.

With so many quality players still at the club there was optimism that Cardiff could regroup and challenge for silverware in the 1926–27 season.

CHAPTER 6

A SEASON TO REMEMBER

Season 1926–27

There was much trepidation among Cardiff fans as the team prepared for the 1926–27 season. While the club still had an abundance of international players on its books, the team's League performance over the last two seasons had been poor. No one could predict whether the team was a mediocre one, destined never to fulfil its potential, or a side that could challenge for the top prizes in the game.

As usual there was a flurry of transfer activity at Ninian Park before the season commenced, with many notable first-team players leaving the club. Jack Evans, the club's first professional player, who had been with Cardiff since 1910, was the first to leave when Bristol Rovers agreed a fee for his signature. Evans had given Cardiff 16 years of fantastic service and in that time he had been virtually an ever present in the side until the signing of George McLachlan the previous season.

Another player to surprisingly depart Ninian Park that summer was former record signing Joe Cassidy, who signed for Dundee. Cassidy had only been with Cardiff since October 1925, but despite scoring a hat-trick on his debut, he had struggled to find his form. It was later revealed that during his time at previous club Bolton, he had lost 22lbs due to severe influenza and although his health had improved at Cardiff, he still lacked stamina and this had affected his performances.

The club captain, Jimmy Blair, was also moved on when he signed for south-coast club Bournemouth for the sum of £3,900. As a result of Blair's departure Fred was asked to lead the side. When Fred had been asked in previous seasons to captain the team in Blair's absence, he had been an inspiration and therefore his appointment was a popular choice. The *Football Echo* said of his promotion to the captaincy: 'A leader in every sense of the word, he commands respect of colleagues and sets an inspiring example by his wholehearted enthusiasm.'

A teammate of Fred's, Ernie Curtis, said of his leadership skills: 'As a captain, he could somehow inspire the whole team. He wouldn't make any fancy speeches but just roll up his sleeves before the kick-off and say: "Come on, get stuck in". Nobody got stuck in more than Fred Keenor. He was all for his club and the supporters loved him.'

It wasn't just Fred's wholehearted efforts on the field that made him the team's natural leader in the eyes of his teammates. Off the field Fred was always very respectful and could be relied upon to provide help and advice in any circumstances; indeed, he would rarely talk about himself and would be eager to know how his teammates were faring. He was also always the life and soul of any party and enjoyed making everyone in the room laugh. It was these attributes that made everyone who came into contact with Fred truly believe that he would run through a brick wall for them and subsequently they would always try that little bit harder to please him on the field, for fear of letting down a man they respected.

The fans of Cardiff City, who were predominantly working class, were also happy to see Fred take over the leadership of the team. Fred had been born in Cardiff and he was already regarded as the unofficial club ambassador, such was his pride in his home town. Furthermore, his rugged, uncompromising, brave style of play embodied the working-class masculine ideal to which the Ninian Park faithful could relate. Many fans of Cardiff City in this era were coalminers, steelworkers or dockers and they appreciated seeing a local boy fight tooth and nail for their side.

Although Fred would have been earning slightly more than the average working man's wage, he was far from prosperous. Consequently his salary did not elevate him to the level where he could not appreciate the everyday struggle of the working classes. Fred's purchases, hobbies and activities were not so different from those who watched him on the terraces at Ninian Park and this helped him remain one of them. This is, of course, a criticism of the modern-day player whose salary is beyond the comprehension of the ordinary working man, and as a result fans and players find it hard to relate to one another.

Fred was also a renowned proud Welshman and quotes such as 'We Welshmen do not mind much if we have to bow the knee to Scotland or Ireland, but we do take a special delight in whacking England' only served to increase his popularity with his many Welsh fans.

Not only was there a new captain in place, but there were also plenty of new arrivals at Ninian Park as Fred Stewart overhauled the squad. He made seven new signings in total during the summer, but neglected to spend big money on any individual; however, some of his budget signings, such as a young local amateur player by the name of Ernie Curtis, would go on to make a big impact at the club.

The *Football Express* was so confident in the team that Fred Stewart had assembled that one of their writers, by the name of 'Pilgrim', wrote a poem dedicated to them:

> I had a little chat today at Ninian Park with Fred: he tells me that he's got a team that's going to beat the band, for George Latham's done his best and got them well in hand.
>
> They haven't spent a lot of cash acquiring players new, although from Scotland's rugged shore they've captured quite a few; there's Baillie and there's Pirie, both as nippy as can be, and Irving, late of Dundee, who was swapped for Cassidy.
>
> The forwards, so Fred told me, will be much about the same, and every indication shows that Fergie's on his game, for in the match last Saturday three times he found the net, and that's a sample of the stuff the fans are going to get.

Both Len and Billy Davies are just spoiling for the fray, and we shall see them on the right again next Saturday, while Potter Smith as inside-left and Mac upon the wing will help to make a great attack with any amount of sting.

The half-back line is up to scratch with Keenor, Sloan and Wake, and men like Blackburn in reserve a vacant place to take; and in this same department I can tell you for I know, the City will be stronger than they were a year ago.

Of all the backs one can most confidently speak, though Nelson had the toughest luck at Ninian Park this week; there's Watson and there's Hardy who will make a clinking pair, and there's also Chard and Jennings who are keen to do their share.

In goal there's Farquharson who's as safe as safe can be, and should he want a half-day off why then my friend you see, they just have to call on Wainwright who will nobly fill the gap, or pass the word for Kneeshaw who is quite a smart young chap.

Yes, Cardiff's gotta team this year, the fans loudly cried, it's going to be Fred Stewart's joy and everybody's pride, and if they don't do something you can punch my blooming head, and I'll give up drinking whiskey and I'll take to tea instead.

They're going to try and wake things up, they're going to have a shot, to win their way through all the rounds and pinch the FA pot; they're going to ginger up the League, they're out to win, and if you'd like to fill my glass I'll drink good luck to them.

'Pilgrim's' prediction that the team could 'win their way through all the rounds and pinch the FA pot' would in time be proved prophetic.

While the team was now in place, many of Cardiff's fans were struggling as all was not well with the economy in South Wales. The old established heavy industries that had been predominantly relied upon, such as coalmining, steel-making, tin-plate manufacture, engineering and shipping had collapsed due to foreign competition, outmoded equipment and the loss of overseas markets. In addition, an over-valued currency meant that British goods were over-priced in relation to those of other countries. All of this drastically reduced the activities of Welsh ports, particularly Cardiff's, and many workers were left unemployed as a result.

Unfortunately, South Wales had few alternative work opportunities to offer those affected by the demise of the basic staple industries. The net result was long-term mass unemployment, bringing with it a declining standard of living.

As the 1926–27 season was due to commence, the miners of South Wales were still in the middle of a bitter strike. The dispute had started as far back as 3 May 1926, due to the Government recommending that the miners' wages be cut. This meant that many of Cardiff's supporters simply could not afford to watch the team play as the season got underway.

The miners eventually returned to work in November but they were forced to work an eight-hour day for 10 shillings – half the pay they had received for one hour less in 1921. At this time it cost one shilling for a standing spectator to watch Cardiff play at Ninian Park. The cost of attending games did not, however, deter some die-hard fans, with many reported to have walked over 20 miles in order to get to Ninian Park as they could not afford the train fare.

It was to be expected that Cardiff would struggle to match their attendances of previous seasons, with many fans unable to afford basic amenities, let alone the cost of a football match. It was therefore imperative that the team started the season well, not only to boost local morale, but to also attract as many people as possible to Ninian Park.

Regrettably, Cardiff once again started the season slowly, winning only one of their first nine games, a 3–1 win over Leeds United. On 25 September 1926, with Fred Stewart desperately trying to find a winning combination, he gave debuts to Jim Baillie, Tom Pirie and local boy Ernie Curtis in the home match against Manchester United. Unsurprisingly, with so many debutants in the team, the Bluebirds crashed to a 2–0 defeat.

On the rare occasion when the team did function properly they were a match for anyone, as was seen when they crushed Sheffield United 3–0. Fred was the

Football Express's Man of the Match that day as the paper waxed lyrical about his performance: 'The strength of the City team was the half-back line in which Keenor played a magnificent game. He was the outstanding player of the match. The City captain and pivot has, judging by his performances today, returned to his best form. He had a very elusive trio to contend with in Gillespie, Johnson and Roxburgh, but he succeeded in completely subduing them and was also able to give his forwards plenty of good support.'

These types of performances by the team were unfortunately few and far between, and with such poor displays, and many fans unable to afford the luxury of attending a football match, attendances slumped. On 20 November 1926 the visit of West Ham United saw a crowd of just 8,000 attend the game.

As New Year approached many squad members were given their chance to impress the Cardiff manager, but the team continued to flatter to deceive. Matters were not helped when Welsh international Willie Davies was confined to a sanatorium after contracting pleurisy, an illness that would keep him out of action for a year.

During this time Fred was suffering with various injuries but typically he had tried to set an example and play on through the pain barrier. Unsurprisingly, his form began to suffer and as a result Fred Stewart had no option but to leave him out of the side for a period.

Fred was very frustrated at being on the sidelines, but he still recognised that the club was more important than any individual and willed Cardiff to win, with or without him; indeed, such was Fred's enthusiasm for Cardiff that it also cost him the price of a new hat: 'I was watching a game from the stand when in one thrilling attack I rose from my seat, and for the moment thought I was taking part in the movement. My demonstration must have been a little too realistic because I hit a spectator's hat into the enclosure, where it was trampled on by the crowd. That cost me the price of a new hat, and the gentleman swore it was a guinea bowler.'

Yet while Fred still wanted Cardiff to win, he felt that at the age of 32 he needed to be playing regular football. Subsequently, in January 1927, he handed in a transfer request to the Cardiff City directors. On 19 January 1927, the directors of the club met at the Corporation pub, in the Canton area of Cardiff, in order to discuss Fred's request. Ironically, it was Walter Riden, Fred's old school teacher and the man who had brought him to the club in 1912, who proposed allowing Fred to leave. This proposal was subsequently seconded and it looked for a time as if Fred would be seeking pastures new.

At one stage Bristol Rovers looked to be on the verge of signing Fred, but the move fell through as he managed to win back his place in the team and recapture his form. Within a matter of weeks Fred was removed from the transfer list so that he could concentrate on helping steer the team towards safety.

With Fred back in the team the Bluebirds' form started to improve. Between 15 January 1927 and 24 March 1927 Cardiff lost just once. Another reason for this run of good form was the signing of winger Billy Thirlaway from Birmingham City. Prior to the capture of Thirlaway, Fred Stewart had been playing record signing Hughie Ferguson on the wing. Thirlaway's presence meant that Ferguson returned to his natural striker's berth, and he responded by firing in 11 goals in his next 12 League games.

Fred's return to the Cardiff defence, and Ferguson's return to the forward line, meant that the Bluebirds were resolute at the back and now scoring freely. Stewart had finally managed to get the balance right in his side and the Bluebirds subsequently rose up the table, where they eventually finished in 14th place.

Once again Cardiff had record signing Hughie Ferguson to thank for another year in the First Division of the Football League. Despite the fact that he had played half the season on the wing, Ferguson had finished the campaign with 25 goals, almost half of the team's total.

Although the Bluebirds had endured another testing season in the League, this was the year where they would finally achieve unprecedented success in the FA Cup, a competition which many felt was more prestigious than the Football League title itself.

On 8 January 1927, Cardiff began their Cup run when they faced Aston Villa at Ninian Park. Cardiff's form had been dismal going into the game, as they had won just twice in their previous nine League games, and they were therefore not fancied to beat the Midlands side. Fred was left out of the team but surprisingly the Bluebirds went on to win 2–1, following goals from Len Davies and Ernie Curtis.

In the next round Cardiff were drawn against Darlington of the Third Division North, whom they had faced during their 1925 Cup run. While on that occasion Cardiff had taken three attempts to dispose of Darlington, this time they did the job at the first time of asking with Hughie Ferguson and George McLachlan scoring the goals in a 2–0 away win.

In preparation for their third-round clash at Bolton Wanderers, the squad stayed in Southport prior to the game. A Cardiff City match programme revealed just how the players spent their time:

> On Tuesday morning they indulged in ball practice, afterwards proceeding to the baths, where they had a hot salt-water bath, followed by a swim in the swimming baths, where, by the way, they enjoyed themselves to their hearts' content. In the afternoon, some went golfing while others indulged in tennis.
>
> On Wednesday, similar training took place, minus the baths, and on Thursday they repeated Tuesday's training again, indulging in a hot sea-water bath.

During the players' round of golf, at the Royal Birkdale golf club, some members of the squad noticed that a small black kitten was following them. The players saw this as a lucky omen and sent centre-forward Hughie Ferguson to locate the kitten's owner in order to broker a deal whereby the team could keep their good luck charm. Ferguson eventually tracked down the owner and struck a deal with him whereby the team could keep the kitten as long as they promised to supply the owner with a Cup Final ticket should they reach Wembley. The team christened the kitten Trixie, and she would remain at Ninian Park until her death in 1939.

Fred was recalled to the side for the Cup tie against Bolton, who were one of the League's form teams, and clear favourites to progress against the struggling Bluebirds; however, just the week before the game, Fred had played in an international for Wales against England in which he had injured Bolton and England centre-half James Seddon with one of his trademark take-no-prisoners challenges. As a result Seddon was ruled out of the game against Cardiff, much to the fury of the Bolton supporters, who barracked Fred at every opportunity. As Fred recalls:

> I was the victim of a noisy demonstration as soon as I entered the field, and every time I went for the ball the crowd howled and jeered.
>
> During the interval Mr Fred Stewart, father, friend and counsellor to all the boys, had a heart-to-heart talk with me. He told me not to take any notice of the spectators, but to continue playing my natural game. I might add that I was in my element in such conditions. The more the crowd shouted, the harder I played.

Indeed, Ernie Curtis also recalled the abuse Fred received in the game and his reaction to it: 'The worse it got the better and harder he played.'

Fred made an inspirational return to the team at Bolton as he captained Cardiff to a surprise 2–0 victory, with the goals again coming from the dynamic duo of Hughie Ferguson and Len Davies.

'Pilgrim', of the *Football Express*, attributed the win over Bolton to the team's good luck charm, Trixie the cat:

> Once more it's up to us to sing
> Of Cardiff City's fame:
> To make the very echo's ring,
> And loud extol their name;
> For Bolton thought to win the round
> And counted not the cost,
> But Ferguson a kitten found,
> And that was why they lost!
> Full fifty thousand Bolton boys,

To help the Wanderers win,
Set up a truly awful noise,
In fact a mighty din;
But all the rattles that they bought,
And all their beastly row,
The City players set at nought,
When Trixie said 'Miaow!'
Though Bolton tried to set the pace
And launched a hot attack,
The City beat them in the race,
And quickly drove them back;
Then when the crowd to cheer were stirred,
I'm quite prepared to vow
That all the City players heard
Was Trixie's faint 'Miaow!'
For Trixie's soft consoling purr
Re-echoed in their ears;
It called to mind her jet black fur,
And silenced all their fears;
It drove away their erstwhile gloom,
For there amid the din,
With Trixie in the dressing room,
They knew that they would win!

Cardiff's reward for their best performance of the season was a quarter-final tie against Chelsea, who were fighting for promotion from the Second Division. Even though some Cardiff fans were still struggling financially it is estimated that 12,000 of them made their way to Stamford Bridge to watch the Bluebirds draw 0–0 with Chelsea.

The game may have not have been a classic, but many of the Cardiff supporters that day had never previously left the confines of South Wales and they therefore enjoyed spending time in the capital. The fans marvelled at the sights and sounds of one of the world's great cities, and many went to watch the Changing of the Guard at Horse Guards Parade in Whitehall, while others enjoyed the bars that the West End had to offer. London would have been a far cry from some of the villages in the valleys where many of Cardiff's fans hailed from.

On the day of the midweek replay, a torrential downpour battered South Wales. The miserable conditions did not deter the Cardiff faithful, however, as over 48,000 supporters braved the elements to attend the game. This was, of course, before the days of all-seater stadiums, stands providing cover and an abundance of convenience outlets. The fans at the game would have been crammed into a pen with no roof, such as the uncovered Bob Bank or Grange End, so that for the duration of the game they would not only have to stand, but would also be at the mercy of the weather.

If you were lucky enough to be at the front of the pen you might have had the advantage of a superior view of the game, but this was outweighed by the problem of reaching the toilets at the back of the stand should you require them. As there was no walkway allowing easy access to the toilets, many fans either urinated on the person in front of them or wet themselves. Therefore you could always guarantee that there would be the stench of cigarette smoke and urine wafting from the stands.

Furthermore, many of the stands at Ninian Park were not only left open to the elements, but were also earth based. Therefore during a downpour the ground beneath you would turn to sludge, caking your shoes and trousers in mud.

Another consideration for the fans was that being drenched for over 90 minutes brought a real risk of becoming ill. At this time antibiotics and many other medicines had yet to be discovered, so catching an ailment such as flu could in fact endanger your life; indeed, if you did fall ill and were unable to attend work, you were also unlikely to be paid, which could see you struggle to buy food for your family while you were off work.

With all these things to consider it is a wonder that so many people did attend football matches on a regular basis. Thankfully, on this occasion, the

Cardiff fans were rewarded for their efforts as the replay against Chelsea turned out to be one of the most dramatic and controversial games ever seen at Ninian Park.

The heavy underfoot conditions forced the Bluebirds to abandon their renowned short passing game and instead implement long-ball tactics. Chelsea had prepared their team to combat Cardiff's short passing and consequently found it difficult to cope with this change of tactics. Due to this, Cardiff shot into an early lead when Len Davies's shot rebounded off the crossbar and Sammy Irving tapped in the rebound. Cardiff then stretched their lead after 20 minutes when Len Davies was on target to put Cardiff two goals ahead.

Fred had been assigned the task of keeping Chelsea's danger man, Andy Wilson, quiet, and he excelled as Wilson hardly had a kick. However, Wilson was soon given an opportunity to make his mark on the game through no fault of Fred's.

Ten minutes before half-time Chelsea were awarded a penalty with Wilson designated to take the kick. Farquharson, the Cardiff goalkeeper, was known as 'the Penalty King' for his outstanding record of penalty saves due to his unusual tactic of standing at the back of the goal and rushing out as the penalty-taker approached the ball. Farquharson had said of this tactic: 'I can move forward before the kick is actually taken, a course I cannot take if I stood on my goalline. By advancing forward I can leap to either side far more quickly than from a standing position.'

Farquharson's strategy worked again as he saved Wilson's penalty virtually on the edge of his six-yard box.

Wilson later said of Farquharson's save: 'I thought I was seeing things when I looked at Tom Farquharson in the Cardiff goal. As I placed the ball, he was standing with his back against the net, outstretched hands gripping the meshes. I shot and he dashed forward and made a wonder save.'

Such was Farquharson's brilliance at saving penalties with this tactic that in 1929 the Football League had to introduce the rule that the goalkeeper's feet must remain on the goalline before a penalty could be taken.

The penalty save would not, however, be the end of the controversy. With just minutes remaining in the first half the Chelsea right-half, Priestley, fired in a shot which appeared to have skimmed the far post and gone off for a goal-kick. But the referee enraged the Cardiff players by awarding a goal as he felt that the ball had gone through the net, which was not being held down by pegs. A watching policeman confirmed to the referee that this was the case and the goal was given, much to the disgust of the Cardiff players.

As the two teams emerged for the second half Cardiff were still seething with injustice. With the players' minds not fully concentrating on the game, Chelsea took advantage by scoring the equaliser five minutes after the restart. Cardiff were by now floundering and Chelsea almost went into the lead when they hit the crossbar. Matters then went from bad to worse as the Bluebirds were reduced to 10 men for a lengthy period, as Ernie Curtis had to leave the pitch to receive treatment to an injury.

Ten-man Cardiff managed to weather the storm, and when Curtis returned to the game, with just seven minutes remaining, it was his late cross that resulted in a penalty being awarded for handball. Hughie Ferguson stepped forward to take the penalty, but such was the state of the pitch that he struggled to find where the penalty spot was amid the mud. After eventually locating it Ferguson kept his nerve and smashed home the winner. Not long after the goal the referee blew the final whistle to spark ecstatic scenes as the crowd invaded the pitch to celebrate the team yet again reaching the FA Cup semi-final.

Cardiff would once more have to overcome Second Division opponents in the semi-finals when they were drawn against Reading, who had defeated Cardiff's archrivals Swansea Town in the previous round. Before the game the team again retreated to Southport for a week of relaxation. With a stress-free atmosphere, and an improving League position, the Cardiff players were in a confident mood as they made their way to the neutral venue of Molineux for the game.

The Bluebirds started the match in rampant form, in front of a crowd of 39,476, with Ferguson scoring the opening goal in the 25th minute. The lead was then extended when Harry Wake converted a McLachlan cross with a flying header. Ferguson then added to his tally with another goal in the second half as the Bluebirds cruised to a 3–0 win. Despite Cardiff's poor League form they were in the FA Cup Final for the second time in just three years.

The Cardiff half-back line of Hardy, Keenor and Sloan were credited by the *Daily Mirror* as being the key to the victory over Reading: 'Three great half-backs put Cardiff into the Final of the English Cup. Keenor, Sloan and Hardy dominated the semi-final tie. The Reading wingers were always in subjection to Keenor and Hardy. McDonald, perhaps the best forward in the Reading line as a rule, never had a chance with Hardy, who beat him all ends up. Keenor used his weight fiercely but fairly against Robson, with the result that the Reading left wing was hardly seen in the game.'

Fred could not believe that he would have another opportunity to win the FA Cup so soon after losing out in 1925: 'When we were beaten by Sheffield United I thought my chance of getting a winners' medal had gone forever.'

Waiting for the Bluebirds in the Cup Final at Wembley would be Arsenal. The Gunners may be considered one of the biggest teams in Europe today, but in the 1920s it could be argued that Cardiff City were actually the more successful and bigger club by virtue of their previous Cup Final appearance and attempt to win the title in 1924.

Arsenal's League form was not much better than the Bluebirds' that term as they had also struggled to escape mid-table mediocrity. But Arsenal were managed by Herbert Chapman, who had, of course, previously managed Huddersfield when they pipped Cardiff to the Championship, and he would in time revolutionise Arsenal into the force they are known as today.

At this point, however, Chapman had yet to make his mark on the Arsenal team as it had conceded 86 goals that season, a dismal total matched by only four other teams in the top flight. The team had only managed to stay out of trouble by scoring an abundance of goals, with their top scorer, Jimmy Brain, on target a total of 31 times. Brain's goals eventually helped Arsenal finish the season three places above Cardiff City. Ironically, Brain had had a trial at Cardiff seven years previously, when he had been playing for Ton Pentre, but in a rare lapse of judgement Fred Stewart had neglected to sign him.

Arsenal's form, like Cardiff's, had improved in the Cup and they had got to the Final by overcoming Sheffield United, Port Vale, Liverpool, Wolverhampton Wanderers and Southampton. This was the first Cup Final that the team had reached and therefore, unlike Cardiff, they had never had the opportunity to play at Wembley before. There was little to choose between the two mid-table sides. Arsenal were better in attack, while Cardiff were superior in defence; indeed, Arsenal captain Charlie Buchan said of Cardiff's defence, which was of course marshalled by Fred: 'I only hope that it will prove to be the weak link in the chain, otherwise we seem to be up against an impassable barrier.'

As in previous rounds, the Bluebirds had once more retired to their retreat in Southport in order to prepare for the game. On 22 April 1927 the team made its way to London by train, with their lucky black kitten Trixie in tow. Upon the team's arrival in the capital the club's entourage divided into two; the players set off to stay at the King's Head hotel in Harrow, while the City officials went to the Palace Hotel in Bloomsbury. Cardiff were by this stage well versed in Cup Final preparation after the experience of the 1925 Final.

However, both Cardiff and Arsenal had injury worries before the game. Just one week before the Final, Harry Wake, who had been blamed for the Sheffield United goal in the 1925 Final, had sustained kidney damage in Cardiff's win against Sheffield Wednesday and would not be fit for the game. Wake's absence from the team would mean that local boy Ernie Curtis, just 19 years old, would deputise and in the process become the youngest person ever to have played in a Cup Final at that point.

Arsenal's injury concerns were far worse as they were facing the prospect of being without three of their first team. Full-back Horace Cope was ruled out with a knee injury while right-half Alf Baker and outside-left Sid Hoar faced a late fitness test to determine whether they would make the starting line up at Wembley. Both Baker and Hoar did play in the Final after successfully proving their fitness.

As always, Fred was mindful in the run-up to the Final that the club was not just representing the city of Cardiff, but also the whole of Wales, in attempting to become the first-ever Welsh team to win the FA Cup. As on previous occasions, when he had spoken of Cardiff City representing Wales when they were elected into the Football League, Fred spoke only of bringing the FA Cup back to Wales and not specifically to Cardiff. It was comments such as this that saw Fred become popular not only with fans of Cardiff City, but also with fans of their rivals, such as Swansea Town and Newport County.

Shortly after 1pm on the day of the Final, the Bluebirds started to make their way to their date with destiny. They were driven from their hotel to Wembley in a charabanc decorated with a leek emblem on the bonnet, which was surmounted by a small red-dragon flag with blue and white streamers. The players calmed their nerves on the 45-minute journey to the stadium by singing songs.

Unlike in 1925, the players were relaxed as they prepared for the game, having learnt their lesson from their previous appearance. On this occasion the team only arrived at Wembley an hour before kick-off, as the players felt that in 1925 they had arrived too early and had got nervous as a result.

Ernie Curtis said of the 1927 preparations: 'I remember I had no pre-match nerves at all. We had no fear of Arsenal, as our records that season were very similar. We had been to Wembley in 1925 but it was their first visit. We arrived an hour before kick-off. Apparently, in 1925, the team had got to the stadium too early and nerves had affected everyone during the long wait. This time it was different – a sing-song on the journey there and then straight into the dressing rooms.'

In contrast with Cardiff's relaxed journey Arsenal were not as well organised, having never previously had to prepare for an FA Cup Final. The Arsenal team did not set out for Wembley until 1.45pm and as a result they got caught up in traffic congestion and at one point looked likely to miss the 3pm kick-off. In order to avoid this embarrassment, Herbert Chapman had to leave the team charabanc and telephone for a police escort in order to negotiate the team through the crowds and get to the stadium in time for the kick-off.

As the Cardiff team got changed into their strips, Fred, along with fellow senior players Tom Farquharson, Jimmy Nelson and Billy Hardy, gave the team a rousing pep talk. They reminded the players of the hurt of losing the 1925 Final and how many of their fans had made huge sacrifices that season to follow the team, so it was imperative not to let them down.

Unlike today, before 1930 it was a tradition that the teams emerged out of the Wembley tunnel separately. On this occasion it was the Bluebirds who emerged onto the field first in order to be presented to King George V.

Fred was keen to diffuse any tension that his teammates might be feeling, so as they ran out onto the field he broke with tradition by running in front of the team and kicking the ball he had been carrying for the Cardiff players to chase. It is, of course, common to see players these days emerge from the tunnel and kick a football onto the pitch, but it had not been done before Fred did it in the 1927 Final. This breach of protocol calmed the players' nerves, as Ernie Curtis recalled: 'Fred gave us all a gee-up as we prepared and then as we marched out of the tunnel, he gave the ball a mighty kick and we broke rank and charged after it. Arsenal followed out, walking stiffly, but for any of our lads who had been feeling apprehensive, it was just like any other game.'

Fred said of his pre-match tactic: 'I did not mention a word to our manager, Fred Stewart, but I told the lads: "as soon as I get on the pitch I'm going to kick the ball to the halfway line!" I gave it a mighty thump and four or five of us chased after it.'

The players' lack of big-game nerves, thanks in part to Fred, was also noted in the *South Wales News*: 'Spectators of Saturday's game who had witnessed the Final two years ago were agreeably surprised to find that the City on the present occasion, when taking the field, betrayed not the slightest sign of nerves. They galloped on in sprightly fashion, and in contrast to the almost military-like stride of the Gunners, whose progress on the field was in measured tread and slow.'

The fantastic condition of the Wembley pitch, in stark contrast to some of the mud heaps that the players usually played on, also no doubt relaxed the players. Fred said of the conditions: 'Stepping on to the pitch, the first thought that runs through the mind is "If I cannot play football on this magnificent stretch of turf I had better give up the game." Absolutely level, it is the best ever and I am not forgetting such grand pitches as Hampden Park, Fulham and Bury.'

As the two teams lined up Fred presented each of his teammates to King George V. Ernie Curtis said about being presented to the King: 'When Fred Keenor introduced me to the King, he shook my hand and mumbled something indecipherable. When people asked me later what he said, I told them "Hello Ernie, how are you?" "Fine George, see you after the game!"'

Back in the Welsh capital thousands of people gathered to listen to the match in Cathays Park, just outside the City Hall, where specially mounted speakers relayed the first-ever live commentary of an FA Cup Final. This was a real treat for football fans, as if they were not at the match, the only way they would usually know what had happened would be when the *Football Echo* was released shortly after the game had finished. This would result in hoards of football fans crowding around newspaper stands waiting for the first edition to be delivered. However, the sound of the battle at Wembley, over the radio, seemed even more nerve-racking than watching the game itself, or waiting for the newspaper.

As the match got underway it soon became apparent that the game was going to be a tight affair, with Arsenal playing in a surprisingly defensive manner and Cardiff's defence expertly marshalling Arsenal's forwards on the rare occasion that they did attack. The first half passed by with little incident or chances for either team and it appeared as though just one goal would be enough to win the game.

Indeed, Fred later commented on why he felt that most Cup Finals were lacklustre affairs and why many top players failed to perform at Wembley: 'The records show, however, that few footballers do well at Wembley. More reputations are marred than made. Why is this? Many consider that the ceremony has a disturbing effect – the huge crowd, the community singing, the massed bands and the presence of Royalty – all have been quoted as upsetting the players. My own view is that none of these things count to such an extent as the outsider imagines. But quite definitely there is an atmosphere about Cup Final day which militates against a display of good football.'

The game did not improve in the second half and as a result the crowd became tense as the contest was hanging on a knife-edge. As in the 1925 Final, it appeared that either a mistake or a flash of inspiration would be needed in order for the deadlock to be broken.

A hush of silence crept over the ground as for a moment it looked as if Hoar of Arsenal was clean through on goal until Fred heroically saved the day with a last-ditch tackle.

Then, with just 16 minutes remaining on the clock, the moment all of Wales had been waiting for arrived. McLachlan approached the Arsenal penalty area on the left and switched the ball infield to Hughie Ferguson, who stood on the corner of the box. Ferguson managed to get a shot off, but did not connect with the ball as well as he would have liked; however, as the ball bounced off the surface it spun awkwardly. The Arsenal goalkeeper, Dan Lewis, knelt down sideways to gather the ball into his body, with one eye on the advancing Len Davies. Disaster struck for Lewis as he failed to read the spin on the ball and as he gathered it into his chest the ball spun off his jersey and squirmed from his grasp. Lewis panicked, seeing Davies advancing, and as he tried to hurriedly re-gather the ball, his elbow knocked it over the goalline, much to the delight of the Cardiff players and supporters. City were 1–0 up.

The *Football Express* described the scenes inside the stadium after the ball had crossed the line for a goal: 'As one man the Welsh crowd rose and cheered as they had never cheered before. The women lost their heads, and turning to those next to them, threw their arms around them, utterly regardless of the fact that except for the common bond of Wales they were utter strangers.'

The fans listening to the game at Cathays Park also celebrated wildly as the news broke over the radio that Cardiff had scored: 'The wonderful news that Ferguson had scored came so suddenly as to momentarily silence the crowd; then broke forth a mighty roar, such as has rarely been heard in the city before.'

It was Lewis's elbow that finally knocked the ball over the line, but the goal would be credited to Hughie Ferguson. Ferguson later told the *South Wales News*: 'I know that I shot but I did not know whether the ball was touched by anyone else. As we were returning to the centre from the goal area, I spoke to Len Davies and I asked him if he had touched the ball and he replied "No".'

Fred, as ever, would defend his Welsh international teammate Dan Lewis, when he later said of the goal: 'What a lot of people haven't taken into account was how Ferguson had hit the ball. He put such a spin on it that it would have been difficult for the 'keeper to have saved cleanly. The ball twisted in his hands, bounced onto his chest and curled back into the net. Len Davies was challenging and I think Lewis took his eye off the ball for a fatal second as he went down for it at the near post.'

With little time remaining in the game Arsenal were unable to exert any real pressure on Cardiff as Fred stubbornly refused to let the Gunners back into the match. Cardiff were, in fact, unlucky not to double their lead when, with two minutes remaining, Curtis, the baby of the team, cut in from the wing and was presented with virtually an open goal, but somehow shot wide.

As the *Football Echo* revealed, the scenes at Cathays Park were becoming increasingly fraught before the final whistle was blown: 'A sharp snap was heard near me, a man fiddling with a nail file, which had suddenly given way under his nervous grasp. A nearby child started wailing, lending a mournful note above the tense stillness.'

In the dying minutes of the game there was one final moment of drama as the ball was rolled across the Cardiff six-yard box for the Arsenal forward, Hoar, to seemingly tap the ball into an empty net. Fred 'sensationally' flung himself in front of the ball and miraculously it deflected off his body and went out for a corner.

Arsenal failed to capitalise on the resulting corner-kick and moments later the referee blew the final whistle. Cardiff City had historically become the first non-English team to win the FA Cup, on St George's Day of all days! Following the final whistle the scenes of euphoria inside the stadium were chaotic, as the *Football Express* described: 'When the final whistle blew, shrill feminine shrieks mixed with the men's cheers. Men and women swooned over the barricade onto the touchline, and the players underwent what might well have been their most trying experience of all. Men slapped them on their backs; women hugged them;

girls kissed them and sobbed all over them. One elderly lady, how she managed to climb the 4ft concrete barrier is a mystery, went almost crazy with joy.'

The supporters back in Cathays Park were also deliriously happy knowing that their beloved Bluebirds would be bringing the Cup back to Wales with them: 'Then, at last, time was reached, and the knowledge that the Cup had come to Wales at last brought forth the great rejoicing among the crowd. A rush was made towards the city centre, and the news was shouted excitedly, nobody listening, everybody shouting.'

Celebrations broke out throughout the city as the police struggled to contain the giddy scenes: 'In Caroline Street some 200 anxious watchers gathered outside a wireless shop as the game neared its close One old gentleman, holding a watch, counted the minutes and was among the first to lead a great cheer that went up when it became known that the City had won. A perspiring young policeman, whose face was wreathed in smiles, had difficulty in controlling the people as they poured into St Mary Street.'

Back at Wembley the former Welsh Prime Minister, David Lloyd George, led the celebrations as he told the *South Wales News*: 'This is the first Cup tie that I have attended and I was thrilled. It was a splendid game. Both teams fought with British pluck and sportsmanship. I am very pleased that my fellow countrymen have, for the first time, taken the Cup to Wales.'

Besides Cardiff becoming the first and only team from outside of England to win the Cup, the 1927 Cup Final was a first for a variety of reasons. For the first time ever at Wembley the crowd sang the hymn *Abide With Me* before the game. This has become a tradition, as fans at every subsequent Cup Final have sung this anthem.

As stated previously, much to the delight of football fans throughout the country, this was the first FA Cup Final broadcast live on the radio. As a result the phrase 'back to square one' originated here. The *Radio Times* had published a grid of the pitch, with it split up into numbered zones, so that those listening on the radio could understand where the ball was on the field when the commentator said it was in a certain zone. Square one was, of course, in the goal area for each team.

Another notable occurrence at the Cup Final was the Cardiff fans singing the popular song, *I'm Forever Blowing Bubbles*. While West Ham United would eventually claim this song as their own, Cardiff fans are adamant that they were the first to sing it at a football match.

In order to get his hands on the Cup, Fred had first to climb the famous 39 Wembley steps towards the Royal Box, push his way through a throng of excited Cardiff supporters, greet King George V and only then could he finally lift the famous trophy. The boy who at the turn of the century had captained Stacey Road Primary School to a trophy was now the man who had captained Cardiff City to the most coveted Cup trophy in the world.

It is staggering to think that just 17 years before their Cup win the club had not even been professional and had been playing their games on a rubbish tip; indeed, Cardiff had only been members of the Football League for seven years and therefore their rise from obscurity to FA Cup-winners is without comparison.

It is unlikely that this historic event would have been possible without the heroic efforts of the team's captain. After the game, Arsenal captain Charlie Buchan said of Fred's performance that day: 'He had a store of energy which seemed inexhaustible in defending his goal and supplying his forwards with crisp passes.'

Fred attributed his outstanding Cup Final performance to his pair of lucky boots: 'I've got a pair of football boots which are the nightmare of our trainer George Latham and which weigh about four times the weight of any other pair. When I wear these boots, everything goes right – yes I did wear them in the Cup Final – and I pin my luck to them.'

However, Fred was also gallant in victory when he said of the game: 'I think we were very lucky to win because to be candid, I think the Arsenal deserved to do so. It was a very poor game for a Final but we do not expect these matches to provide the most skilful display. So much depends on the result that we get anxious, and I am sure we all were today. I am very glad we have won, if only because we are taking the Cup to Wales for the first time.'

As the Cardiff players and officials celebrated without abandon in their dressing room, Dan Lewis, the Arsenal and Welsh international goalkeeper, took his runners'-up medal out of the box and threw it to the floor, muttering, 'I didn't come here for this'. Lewis was distraught about his unfortunate part in the goal and his mood was not helped by the unfounded rumours that he had let the ball slip through his grasp in order to help his countrymen win the Cup.

Once the dressing-room celebrations had subsided the Cardiff team travelled to the Palace Hotel in Bloomsbury, where they enjoyed a celebratory meal with the directors and their wives. The hotel had been bombarded with congratulatory telegrams from well-wishers from all over the world and many of them were read out at the dinner.

To welcome the victorious team, the hotel had arranged for the dining room to be decked out in the club colours of blue and white, and the floor had been covered with an artificial grass carpet, a replica of the Wembley pitch. Ernie Curtis recalled: 'We had a big celebration dinner that night at the Palace Hotel in Bloomsbury. The room was decked out in blue and white, and wives and officials joined in for a night I will never forget.'

At Paddington, the Great Western Railway had arranged for a band to play on the platform as the Cardiff fans exercised their vocal chords to good effect as they waited for their trains home. Paddington's special 'non-alcoholic' refreshment bar also remained open until long past midnight to help the fans celebrate the momentous victory.

The next day the team went sightseeing in Windsor, and also visited Runnymede and Kempton racecourses, before finally starting the journey home that would see them take the FA Cup out of England for the first and only time in the history of the game.

However, the Cardiff team had not envisioned the scenes that would greet them, not only at Paddington station, but also at Reading, Swindon and Newport, as they took the trophy back to the Principality. As the train left Paddington, Fred held up the FA Cup and shouted at onlookers 'We might let you see it again next year.'

All the down-line stations were decked in blue and white in Cardiff's honour. Every station that the train pulled into was full of football fans wanting to get a glimpse of the historic team. The players had to endure long delays at each station, as the crowds would not disperse until Fred had shown them the Cup and made a short speech.

To escort the team back to Cardiff, three aeroplanes from the Surrey Flying Services picked up the train en route and gave it a guard of honour all the way home.

As the team finally pulled into Cardiff Central Station there was a surge of emotion as Fred, the Cardiff born and bred captain, and his team, emerged from the train to the sound of a band playing *See the Conquering Heroes Come.*

Harry 'H' Parsons, who would go on to become a member of staff and a Cardiff City legend in later years, watched the homecoming parade as a nine-year-old boy. He said: 'My father took me up to the old monument on Custom House Street near the Glamorganshire Canal to watch the team arrive from London. I can remember seeing Fred Keenor holding the Cup out of the window as the train crossed the bridge near the top of Bute Street before pulling into the station.'

Fred would later say about the reception at Cardiff train station: 'When we reached the station pandemonium broke out, but the police and station officials had organized the welcome with a thought for the players, and like the Roman gladiators of old, we were escorted to our chariot, which in those modern days took the form of a charabanc.'

Lord Mayor Alderman William Grey was waiting at the station to meet the triumphant team and escort them to the City Hall for a civic reception. Cardiff was bursting at the seams as 250,000 people were estimated to be present to applaud Wales' first FA Cup winners.

The drive through the densely-packed streets saw some of the most remarkable scenes in Cardiff's history. Bands preceded the procession of charabancs that carried the official party to the City Hall. Balconies and windows were festooned in blue and white, and supporters gathered on advertisement hoardings and house roofs to cheer themselves hoarse. During the journey to the City Hall, Fred had to stand on a precarious perch giving everyone as good a view of the FA Cup as he possibly could.

Whole families had come from far and wide to cheer the team, including a white goat; the property of a fan from Canton called Charlie Manley, who had walked the length and breadth of England to watch the Bluebirds' away games. Naturally, the animal was decked in blue and white and continually rubbed its head against the side of the charabanc containing the players.

The police were hard pressed to hold back the enthusiastic supporters intent on mobbing their heroes. The biggest problem occurred as the procession was halfway down St Mary Street, when the temporary crush barriers positioned there gave way, resulting in a claustrophobic jam, which required police and Red Cross intervention.

As the Cardiff team stood on the balcony of the City Hall, the Lord Mayor introduced each of the players to loud cheers from the adoring crowd. Onlookers burst into a spontaneous rendition of the Welsh national anthem, and even Trixie the cat was present in blue and white ribbons, as Hughie Ferguson held her in his arms. The biggest cheer of the day, however, came when Fred held the trophy aloft for the crowd to see.

The players were staggered by the reception they had received. An overawed Fred said: 'The Cup was worth winning if only to get a reception like this.'

Englishman Billy Hardy, clearly taken aback, said: 'I have never seen anything like it in the whole of my career. The scenes at Cardiff when we were escorted in triumph through the crowded and decorated streets to the City Hall will remain one of the most glorious memories of my career.'

Irishman Tom Sloan compared the scenes favourably to ones he had seen in his home country: 'St Patrick's Day in Ireland wasn't in it. The reception! The cheering!'

Following the ecstatic scenes, the Cardiff entourage retired inside the City Hall for a dinner and a dance. All the tables were decorated in the club colours of blue and white. During the dinner, films were shown reliving the Wembley victory and tributes were paid to manager Fred Stewart, trainer George Latham and chairman Walter Parker. Messages of congratulations continued to pour in from all over the world from as far afield as the Suez Canal, where the Welsh Regiment were stationed.

Fred revealed after the dinner just how much the Cup win meant to him and the fellow players who were also from Cardiff: 'That evening I was the proudest man in the world, for I was born within the City itself. Len Davies and Ernie Curtis also were locals and no doubt shared my pride.'

The dance was scheduled to finish at 2am but the celebrations continued throughout the week; however, the team still had League fixtures to complete, with Everton visiting Ninian Park the next Saturday. In the programme for the Everton fixture it said: 'Time will pass, new men will appear and those who have managed the club will pass away, but we venture to believe that it will be long before they will be forgotten, for they have carved themselves a niche in the history of sport in Wales which can never be erased.'

Fred Stewart had the luxury of sending out an experimental side against Everton and therefore opted to play Fred at centre-forward. Fred made the most of his chance in the forward line as he signed off the season in style when he duly scored the game's only goal. Yet this feat was not enough to give the FA Cup-winning captain the headlines, which bizarrely read 'Six Year Old Boy Stars for City'. Apparently during the game a six-year-old boy had run onto the pitch and tackled one of the Everton players, much to the crowd's delight.

While Fred missed out on making the headlines on that occasion, one local newspaper showed the high regard the country had for him when it printed a cartoon of the Cardiff City captain knocking former Welsh Prime Minister, Lloyd George, off a pedestal labelled 'The most important man in Wales'. Fred had cemented himself in the hearts of Cardiff City and Wales fans forever with his Cup-winning exploits.

The *South Wales News* perhaps best summed up the team's achievement when it said: 'The sentiment of Wales — and sentiment is more often right than it gets credit for — hailed the Final as in the nature of an international struggle. To the people it was more than a struggle between two teams; it was a struggle between the two nations. This may not be exactly logical but sentiment transcends logic. So this year's Cup Final will remain in consideration a Welsh victory. In conclusion we can express on behalf of all our readers our pride and satisfaction in the whole Cardiff City team, whose success has given an added prestige to Welsh sport by their clever, clean and incisive football.'

For the majority of the players the Cup Final win would be the highlight of their careers. Most of them would not be fortunate enough to win such a prestigious prize again. Ernie Curtis came close when he was a member of the Birmingham team who lost out to West Bromwich Albion in the 1931 Cup Final, while full-back Jimmy Nelson was the only player to win the Cup again when he played for Newcastle in their Cup win over Arsenal in the 1932 Final.

Just 12 days after the Cup Final win Cardiff continued their winning ways when the team beat Rhyl in the Welsh Cup Final 2–0, with Sam Irving and Len Davies the goalscorers; however, the season would be remembered for their historic FA Cup win and it seemed that the Bluebirds were on the brink of becoming one of the elite sides in the country. However, the Cup Final win would prove to be a false dawn, as the club has never yet achieved such dizzy heights again.

CHAPTER 7

THE BITTER DECLINE

Season 1927–28

There was a hive of activity surrounding the club as it prepared for the commencement of the 1927–28 season. With the FA Cup proceeds burning a hole in the directors' pockets, such as the £40 royalties the club had received from Columbia Records as their share of the records sold of the community singing at Wembley, it was decided to spend the windfall on constructing a cover for the Grange End stand at Ninian Park. This project resulted in Fred Stewart having little money at his disposal with which to purchase new players. Subsequently, transfer activity was limited at Ninian Park.

In the match programme for the team's opening game of the season against Bolton Wanderers, the editor expressed his opinion that the team had not required any new players in any event: 'We have no hesitation in expressing the belief that the coming season will prove an even better one than last, for never in the history of the club has it been so well placed for players as at present. In former years, we have signed on a number of new men to strengthen the club's resources. This season, not a single new player of note has been added to the playing strength, a testimony in itself of the satisfaction of the directors with the men at their disposal.'

The summer of 1927 was not only a busy one on the football front for Fred, as he led the team on a tour of Wales in order to show off the Cup, but it was also a busy one on the family front as Muriel Keenor gave birth to their fourth child, Nancy. Fred was particularly proud of his ever-growing family and revealed in an interview that Gladys was very bright and performing well in school, Frederick enjoyed drawing and Alfred spent all his time with a football and was particularly useful in goal for one so young.

It was a period of contentment for Fred with him enjoying family life, revelling in being an FA Cup-winner and back playing some of the best football of his career. At this point in time Fred was renowned as being one of the finest defenders in the Football League, despite standing at just 5ft 7in tall, and not being a particularly skilful player, he could still read the game better than anyone. And if all else failed, the intimidation factor of being on the end of one of Fred's fearsome challenges was enough to keep any player in check. It was said: 'He might not be a stylish player, but his doggedness and determination makes him one of the most effective centre-halves in the country.'

Indeed, such was the esteem in which he was held in the game that several leading English sides tried to pry Fred away from Ninian Park by offering him various financial inducements; however, with Fred playing regularly for the team he loved he admitted that no amount of money could compensate him for leaving.

The atmosphere at the club was still buoyant following the Cup Final win and the players were approaching the new season with real confidence. On 27 August 1927, Fred gave a journalist from the *Sports Budget* a tour around Ninian Park as he discussed the wonderful team spirit and unique conditions at the club:

> Let me show you around Ninian Park, where we are preparing for the new season. After winning the FA Cup in April we have had a hectic summer I can tell you. As captain, I have eaten more free suppers than I ever imagined possible but I am ready for Bolton Wanderers at Ninian Park this Saturday.

Doesn't the ground look a picture. It hardly seems possible that it was a rubbish tip in 1910 – but it was! Today Ninian Park holds 60,000, the concrete stand cost £8,000 and we are having another built in the near future. The pitch is looked after by old David Gouldstone, an excellent groundsman. He has to suffer a lot of leg-pulling, but he's an old soldier and takes it well. Dave likes a bet but none of the lads have made a fortune from his tips.

The chap with that big cheery grin is George Latham. Everyone knows George and the dog with him is Bonzo, his pet bull-terrier who doubles-up as a night watchman. Wait until you see our dressing room. George keeps it full of flowers and his eight canaries are always in good voice.

The players will be coming in for a massage soon. We call Jim Nelson and Tom Watson the Siamese Twins. Always together and always up to no good! One of their favourite tricks is to wait until we are all in the showers and then turn on the cold water. And when we stay away they regularly manage to sew up one of the lads' pyjamas! Quite a few of the lads like a game of snooker or billiards and you'll often find Len Davies, Ernie Curtis, Billy Hardy and myself on the table in the recreation room. But our billiards prize must go to Sam Irving, who also enjoys a game of golf. We've got several musicians at the club. Jack Jennings, Ernie Curtis and Harry Wake can all tinkle the ivories a bit, while Tommy Sloan thinks he is the best singer in all of Cardiff. Tommy Farquharson is a keen dancer, always up to the latest fads, and he claims to be able to pick up any music station in the world on that wireless of his. Hughie Ferguson and George McLachlan also have musical tastes but of the gramophone variety. Both claim to be keen collectors and George, like myself, is a motorist. Harry Wake is a good friend of mine and acts as a secretary of the Cardiff City Benevolent Fund, a scheme originated by the directors, by which the players subscribe now and again for the poor and needy of the Cardiff district. I don't know whether any other clubs practice the same sort of idea: I haven't heard of any who do.

Winning the FA Cup was a great ambition of mine. I pledged our return after losing to Sheffield United in 1925. My sympathies then went out to dear old Harry who was unfairly blamed for our defeat. Then fate capped it all when Harry was injured and had to miss the Final success over Arsenal. I think it helped spur the boys on to victory. As a Cardiff boy, I was overwhelmed with our home-coming, and Len Davies, Ernie Curtis and myself felt ever so proud to be natives of this great City. The scenes outside City Hall will remain with us long after our playing days are over.

The feel-good factor around Ninian Park was boosted even further when Cardiff started the season in scintillating form. They followed their opening day 2–1 home win over Bolton Wanderers by not losing in the next six games. This run would eventually be humiliatingly broken when Huddersfield mauled Cardiff in an 8–2 defeat.

Just two days after the Huddersfield game a weary Cardiff team travelled to Scotland in order to face Scottish Cup-winners Glasgow Celtic at Hampden Park. Only 6,000 fans turned out to watch the exhibition game as Cardiff crashed to another heavy defeat, this time losing 4–1.

Notwithstanding these poor away results, the team's home form was particularly strong during the 1927–28 season and this meant that the Bluebirds spent all of the campaign in the top 10. Such was Cardiff's home form that when Huddersfield visited Ninian Park the Bluebirds avenged their 8–2 defeat from earlier in the season when they won 4–0. Fred was also in fine form, the *Football Express* commenting that he was a 'shining light' in the team.

The South Wales economy was still in deep decline at this time, which unsurprisingly resulted in low attendances, as the *Football Echo* reported: 'Large sections of the crowd are drawn from outlying districts, and comprise enthusiasts who, in previous seasons were regular visitors, but who now, on the score of the economy, so they say, content themselves with a visit to selected games. All along comes the plea from club officials, "Give us better support, and we, in turn, will provide you with attractive football through improved teams." Then comes the inevitable retort, "Give us better-class football and we will support the local club.'"

The drop in attendances meant that Fred Stewart was forced to wheel and deal throughout the season, with the club selling star players such as Ernie Curtis to Birmingham City, Sam Irving to Chelsea and Willie Davies to Notts County. To replace these players Stewart signed Bill Roberts from Flint Town, Matthew Robinson from Pelaw, Tom Helsby from Runcorn and Frank Harris from Cradley Heath. These were hardly the big-name signings the Cardiff fans craved to replace their departing stars and as a result attendances dropped further.

While Cardiff had been in touch with the title-chasing pack, their challenge began to fall apart at the start of the New Year with the forwards misfiring in front of goal. In a I–I draw with Sheffield Wednesday the *Football Echo* reported how Fred tried to rally the Cardiff front line: 'That the Cardiffians, so far as the forwards are concerned, are difficult to weigh up was evidenced by the feeble exhibition in the second half, and not without reason did Keenor exercise his right as a captain in calling upon the raiders to pull themselves together. He set all an example – as a matter of fact, he was an outstanding figure throughout.'

Things then went from bad to worse as Cardiff collapsed during a disastrous March, when they lost 5–I to West Ham and then 7–I at Derby County. The fans were understandably upset at Cardiff's loss of form and the *Football Echo* agreed with their concerns: 'Recent happenings have helped to swell the list of disgruntled enthusiasts. They are exacting, they tolerate nothing less than the best, and make no allowance for sudden loss of form by players whose achievements they often have cheered to the echo. Rightly is the team that holds a commanding position for more than a season or so described as a "wonder team", and deservedly were the Cardiffians included in that category; but the reputation they have gained for themselves is now the standard by which they are judged, and they have fallen from grace. That the collapse is but a passing phase is the devout hope of all concerned with the reputation of Welsh football.'

In the end Cardiff finished the season in the comfort of sixth place, which was a big improvement on their League position in the previous two seasons. There were, however, a few warning signs that all was not well at the club with the team managing to score 70 goals yet uncharacteristically conceding 80. The team was also an ageing one, with Billy Hardy aged 36 and Fred having turned 33.

Cardiff City's defence of the FA Cup began on 14 January 1928 when they were drawn to play Southampton. Len Davies and Hughie Ferguson scored the goals as the Bluebirds won the game 2–1.

Next up for Cardiff was a home tie against Liverpool. In horrendous conditions Cardiff fought back from going a goal down to win the game 2–1, with George McLachlan and Jimmy Nelson getting on the score sheet.

Cardiff were in good form as they travelled to the City Ground to face Nottingham Forest in the next round. However, this would be the day that the blue and white ribbons would be taken off the Cup as Cardiff lost 2–1 in a highly controversial game.

City had taken the lead through Hughie Ferguson, but Forest equalised via the penalty spot when Jimmy Nelson was harshly adjudged to have fouled Forest's Wadsworth. There was further controversy concerning Forest's winning goal as the ball had appeared to go out for a goal-kick and as the Cardiff players stopped, the ball was pulled back into the box for Stocks to score. The Cardiff team vehemently appealed but it was in vain, and the Cup-winners were out of the competition.

On 5 March 1928 the trophy was returned to the FA headquarters at Russell Square. In a simple ceremony, the case was unlocked, the Cup was inspected, and a receipt was issued to the club. No one could have known then that Cardiff would fail to get their hands on the trophy for a period exceeding 80 years.

Cardiff's defence of the Welsh Cup was more successful, however, when they comfortably defeated Bangor City in the Final. The team cruised to a 2–0 victory with Hughie Ferguson scoring the two goals.

As FA Cup-winners the team also participated in the Charity Shield that season. In those days the winners of the FA Cup would play the winners of the amateur cup competition. Cardiff therefore faced the famous amateur side Corinthians at Stamford Bridge. The amateurs surprisingly took the lead in an entertaining game and it was not until 12 minutes from time that Ferguson levelled the scores. Then, with just five minutes remaining, Davies grabbed the winning goal.

All in all it had been a successful season for the Bluebirds. They had finished sixth in the League and had won the Welsh Cup, as well as the Charity Shield.

Further silverware was added to Fred's collection when he again captained Wales to the title in the Victory International Championship. On their way to the Championship Wales dropped just the one point in a game against Scotland, which ended 2–2. In this game Keenor was the outstanding player on the pitch and one report said: 'How Wales would have fared without his leadership is best left to the imagination'.

Despite Fred scoring an own-goal in the international against England, he again delivered an outstanding individual performance as Wales won 2–1. The Championship was once again clinched in Belfast when the Revd Hywell Davies (Davies was the Rector of Denbigh and had played for Corinthians and Wrexham) helped Wales to a 2–1 win.

Cardiff City had organised another overseas tour for the team to undertake as soon as the season had finished. This time they would travel to Denmark where they would take on the crack Danish teams in exhibition games.

The Bluebirds were too strong for their Danish opposition as they defeated Aarhaus 2–0, Aalborg 4–0 and Odense Combination 4–1. The tour was also notable for the fact that substitutes were allowed to be used during the matches, a rule which had not yet been implemented in the Football League.

Fred would always remember the game against Odense in particular due to the Danish side fielding a 'remarkable' young forward by the name of Jensen. Jensen had by all accounts had a very impressive game against Cardiff and Fred conjured up the following superlatives to describe the young Dane's performance: 'He practically played us on his own. His ball control, heading, passing and positioning combined to make him the ideal inside-forward, and we all went in raptures over this second edition of Alex James.'

The manager, Fred Stewart, had also been blown away by Jensen's display and immediately after the game signed the player for Cardiff City, subject to a work permit. Unfortunately for Jensen, and Cardiff City, the Ministry of Labour rejected the work permit application and so Jensen did not become the first foreign player to have ever worn the famous blue shirt of Cardiff City.

Season 1928–29

With another successful season under their belt Cardiff appeared to be a team on the rise, so no one could have predicted the disastrous season that lay in store. Over the summer the Grange End cover at Ninian Park, which had been paid for with the 1927 FA Cup proceeds, was finally finished and Fred Stewart again dabbled in the transfer market. Stan Davies arrived at the club from Birmingham City, but would only have a short stay at Ninian Park before departing to become player-manager of Rotherham United. Other new signings were Emlyn John from Mid-Rhondda and Leslie Jones from Aberdare.

Cardiff City, and in particular Hughie Ferguson, began the season promisingly when Ferguson got off the mark in a 1–1 draw at Newcastle. Then, in the first home game of the season, the team marked the opening of the new Grange End with their biggest-ever win in the First Division when they beat Burnley 7–0. Hughie Ferguson gave a goalscoring masterclass as he scored five of the team's seven goals. At this stage Cardiff looked like they would be real contenders for the Championship.

However, after such a promising start, Cardiff won only one game between 22 September and Boxing Day. The game that Cardiff did win, a 1–0 win over Portsmouth at Fratton Park, was the last away game that the team won that season.

The loss of form could be partly attributed to an injury crisis that gripped Ninian Park as Jimmy Nelson, Tom Watson and Tom Sloan all succumbed to long-term injuries. Hughie Ferguson, the team's talismanic striker, also struggled with niggles throughout the campaign and as a result only featured in 20 games. These were all international-class players and Cardiff did not have enough quality in the squad to replace them while they were incapacitated.

During this time Fred, for so long the idol of Ninian Park, was playing poorly and receiving criticism. Much to his dismay, some fans who had once sung his name now wrote letters to the local press blaming him for Cardiff City's declining form. Fred was by now 35 and his best years seemed to be coming to an end.

Fred Stewart tried desperately to replace his injured and ageing stars. He firstly went out and signed former England international Frank Moss from Aston Villa and then signed the top scorer in the Scottish League, Jim Munro, from St Johnstone. Unfortunately, these signings could not halt the Bluebirds' alarming slide towards the relegation zone.

From 19 January 1929, after a rare home win, when the team beat Derby County 3–0, Cardiff then went the rest of the season with only one further victory, a 3–1 win against Sheffield Wednesday. Fred blamed bad luck for the team's run of form and tried to rally the crowd to get behind the team: 'We are not bemoaning our fate and complaining at Ninian Park…just that little bit of luck which is needed will assuredly come along and our star will then be in its ascendancy. To our supporters I would say: This is the testing time of true support, both morally and financially. Don't be found wanting.'

But the team's poor form could not be attributed to bad luck alone. The team's problem was scoring goals, particularly when Ferguson was injured. Due to this, the team only managed to score a meagre 43 goals, and they failed to score in 17 of their matches that season. Hughie Ferguson had weighed in with 14 goals in just 20 games and Cardiff would be left to rue his absence. Cardiff's defence was still as strong as ever, however, with the team conceding just 59 goals, which meant that the Bluebirds actually had the best defence in the First Division. This made a mockery of the criticism directed towards Fred.

Unbelievably, just two years after winning the FA Cup, and just four years after missing out on the title to Huddersfield, the Bluebirds were relegated from the First Division. Fred would later blame the financial circumstances at Ninian Park which meant they were unable to buy the players that were needed to keep the team up: 'It was a period of great difficulties and the directors were induced to transfer some of their best players. Jennings, Warren, McLachlan,

Irving, Nelson and Hillier were some of the stalwarts who joined other clubs at substantial fees, but even then there was not sufficient money to rebuild the team to the old standard. I am firmly convinced that Cardiff City would have weathered the storm had the circumstances compelling the transferring of players been absent.'

Things did not improve in the FA Cup either as the Bluebirds slumped to their record defeat in the competition when Aston Villa hammered them 6–1. In a sad coincidence, the referee of Cardiff's most humiliating time in the Cup had also refereed the team's finest hour, the 1927 Cup Final at Wembley.

In keeping with the miserable season Cardiff even managed to get humiliated in the Welsh Cup when, despite fielding a strong team, they lost 3–0 to Connah's Quay in the Final.

The players would welcome the end of the sorry campaign and the directors would be left to regret building the new Grange End stand instead of providing Fred Stewart with significant transfer funds with which to strengthen his ageing side.

During the season Fred also took part in one of the more painful games that he would play in his career. Before an international game in Scotland Fred had managed to injure his neck. As the injury occurred just a few hours before the game, the Welsh manager Ted Robbins was unable to call-up a replacement and it looked as if the Wales team might have to take the field with just 10 men. Ever the proud Welshman, Fred was determined that this would not be the case so he arranged to be examined by a doctor to see if anything could be done so that he could play.

'I was rushed off to a doctor, who, after examination, bound me with sufficient adhesive strapping to cover a mummy. Most of it was around my neck, and then the doctor calmly told me that on no account must I jump or head the ball. A centre-half instructed not to jump or head – it was really too funny for words. I gave my consent knowing full well that I could not keep my word, but I was in agony throughout.'

Despite playing through the pain barrier, Fred was unable to help the Welsh team to a win as they lost 4–2.

While the season was a miserable one on a professional level for Fred, he did have cause to celebrate yet another addition to the Keenor clan when Muriel gave birth to their fifth child, Brinley, on 7 December 1928.

Following Cardiff's foreign tours to Czechoslovakia and Germany, Fred had not been particularly fond of going abroad, but he was grateful to be among the Welsh squad that summer when it embarked on its first-ever international tour to Canada. The team travelled to North America via boat, and Fred said of the journey: 'Our first two days at sea were like a nightmare and most of us spent the time in our bunks wishing that the ship would go down. But we soon recovered our sea legs and took part in the many activities with the rest of the passengers. The team, pooling their spare cash, took part in the daily sweep on the mileage covered and we scooped the pool on occasion. After this we took part in the sweep every day, and our net winnings amounted to £25.'

Once Fred arrived in Canada he could not believe the quantity and quality of food that was on offer, particularly since he had always hated the food he had eaten in Europe when on tour with Cardiff City. Subsequently Fred and the team set about enjoying as much of the fare as they could, with a diet that would make nutritionists at professional clubs today cringe: 'On the long train journeys it seemed as if we were feasting all day. This is how a couple of the lads started off with breakfast: Porridge, mixed grill of ham, eggs, sausage and tomatoes, followed by strawberries and cream and ending up with three rolls and butter.'

On the tour the Welsh team crammed in 15 matches in the space of 34 days, yet despite this punishing schedule they still managed to win every game. They also managed to score an incredible 63 goals in these contests, while only conceding 11.

As the statistics above tell you, most of the games were won handsomely, but it was not always an easy ride. At Hamilton, where they won 1–0, play became a little rough and at one stage the crowd invaded the pitch to surround Welsh player Moses Russell. As Fred recalls:

'After about 40 minutes play a terrific struggle took place in our goalmouth during which one of the Hamilton forwards was injured. Immediately hundreds of spectators invaded the field and crowded around Moses Russell, who was in no way to blame for the incident.

'The situation looked very ugly and imagine our alarm when one chap pulled out a revolver and threatened to put an end to our little trip. Police came to our rescue and the gunman was escorted off.

'After the game, however, the crowd waited for Moses Russell but we had smuggled him away and he rejoined us at the station.'

Another game the team found to be tough was when they played West Minster Royals in Vancouver. Wales won the game 2–1, thanks to a late goal, but Fred was surprised at just how fit and quick the Canadian team had been.

However, in one of the easier games on the tour, Wales beat Maitland XI 8–0, with Len Davies scoring seven. Fred felt that, while the tour was an enjoyable experience, the standard of the football was not particularly high and in most cases a good English Second Division side would have beaten the top Canadian opposition comfortably.

Fred and the Welsh team were a big draw with fans and players alike during their time in Canada. In one game against Edmonton, a young player travelled over 500 miles in order to play against them and he then began to travel back home just 15 minutes after the final whistle.

The players also managed to fit in a taste of North American culture as they all went to watch their first baseball game in Toronto, although Fred would not stay to see the end: 'My seat was between two elderly ladies, and one of them, assuming that I was completely ignorant of the game, started to initiate me into its mysteries. Then they quarrelled among themselves and I must confess that I did not stay to watch the end of my first baseball match.'

The Welsh team were frustrated during their stay in Canada by the fact that prohibition was in force and therefore they were unable to purchase any alcohol. That is until one day, in the lounge of the team hotel, a man offered to sell the players a crate of whiskey for the sum of $120, a huge amount back then. The players could not afford this exorbitant sum and reluctantly turned the man away.

There was also embarrassment all round when the team visited the Welsh community in the town of Regina and were asked to give a speech in the Welsh language. As Fred was captain of the team he was expected to speak but he did not know a word of Welsh, and it soon became apparent that neither did any of the team.

The trip to Canada was one of the few foreign tours that Fred enjoyed and it certainly allowed him to take his mind off the troubles of Cardiff City; however, on his return home he would have to get used to the fact that his days of playing top-flight football were at an end.

Season 1929–30
Cardiff had started the decade as a promising, youthful team in the First Division yet they ended it as a declining force in English football's second tier. The ageing team required new reinforcements, but due to being relegated the club did not have any money to spend.

In order to raise funds, Hughie Ferguson, Cardiff's star striker, was sold to Dundee. Ferguson had been worth every penny of his record transfer fee, as not only did he score the winner in the 1927 Cup Final, but he also scored an incredible 76 goals in just 117 League appearances for Cardiff City.

Ferguson's move to Dundee would, however, end in tragic circumstances. As had been the case in his final season at Ninian Park, Ferguson continued to struggle with injury during his time at Dundee. Unfortunately, his form also deserted him as he lost his scoring touch and the fans turned against him.

On 14 December 1929, Ferguson was dropped from the team and tragically, just one month later, he was dead at the age of 31. The barracking by the home supporters had become too much for such a proud man as Ferguson to sustain. On 9 January 1930, after a training session at Dens Park, Ferguson committed suicide by gassing himself. He had hinted at the effect that barracking crowds had had on him when he answered the question, 'What is your message to spectators today?' and he said: 'Be assured that we players are impressed on the field both by your cheers and jeers. Of the former, never tire, the latter – well, sportsmen never resort to it, and they are the only people who matter in sport.'

Ferguson's death was a huge shock to the supporters, officials and players at Ninian Park. He had been a much loved member of the team, not only for his goalscoring heroics, but also for his proud, determined and upbeat demeanour. During his time at the club the *Football Express* had said of him: 'Cardiff City have never had a more loyal or gentlemanly player than Ferguson – he is probably the most popular member of the team because of it.'

Hughie Ferguson would forever be immortalised in the hearts of all Cardiff City fans, gone but most certainly not forgotten. He remains to this day one of just seven players in the entire history of the English and Scottish Football Leagues to have scored over 350 League goals.

Before this tragedy Fred Stewart was able to spend a small amount of money on new players, thanks in part to the transfer fee the club had received for Ferguson. He subsequently brought amateurs and semi-professionals into the club such as Albert Valentine from Southport, William Bird from Llandrindod Wells, Paddy Moore from Mulingar and Wilf Lievesley from Wigan Borough. Cardiff still boasted veteran stars such as Fred, Tom Farquharson, Billy Hardy, Harry Wake and Len Davies, but all of them were approaching their mid-30s with their best days behind them.

With an ageing team, and no new signings of any note, Cardiff unsurprisingly lost their opening game against Charlton Athletic 4–1. While Cardiff won the following game against Preston North End 2–0 they lost the next to Hull, and this was a pattern that occurred throughout the season.

The fans were frustrated by their inconsistent team, who were brilliant one game and then hopeless the next, and Fred began to take the brunt of their criticism. The *Football Express* interviewed Billy Hardy and enquired about the fans' shabby treatment of their former hero:

> I asked Billy Hardy why it was that Fred Keenor was apparently so little appreciated by Ninian Park patrons. 'I cannot understand it,' said Hardy, 'Fred is a marvel; one of the greatest-hearted players I have known, and make no mistake about it, we have not a centre-half to compare with him. I would do no more than ask City supporters to remember this, for never were truer words spoken by one player of another. Keenor is playing well, the whole team are playing well, and

Cardiff City will, if given the support and encouragement they deserve, win far more matches than they will lose.'

This was without a doubt Fred's lowest moment in his career as a professional footballer. It was the first time that the Cardiff fans had really turned against him and it came during a period when Fred himself questioned his ability. After a 1–0 home defeat to Hull City, Fred's fighting spirit was temporarily crushed as the Cardiff fans blamed him for the team's appalling defensive display and showered him with abuse. As Fred returned to his Whitchurch home he was obviously upset and seriously considered retiring. As usual it was Muriel who consoled him and convinced him to continue. It was not very often that Muriel would see Fred so downhearted, but the catcalls from the fans who once chanted his name cut him deep.

Sadly, it was not just the Cardiff fans who abused Fred. In one match away at old adversaries Tottenham Hotspur, one of his trademark challenges injured one of their players. The *Football Echo* reporter at White Hart Lane said that he had never seen such merciless abuse directed towards one player as it was at Fred that day:

Keenor, after the injury to O'Callaghan, the Ebbw Vale boy, in the first half, was subjected to merciless baiting by the crowd. The Tottenham spectators, in fact, demonstrated to a surprising and uncalled for extent.

Never have I been so disgusted at a football match. Poor old Keenor went through the mill as he has never been through it before in the whole extent of his distinguished career.

A Tottenham player expressed himself thus: 'The crowd can bait Keenor as much as they like, but they cannot get away from the fact that he is still a class centre-half.'

Fred was not the only player who was subject to the Cardiff crowd's displeasure, as most of the team were heavily criticised for not coming up to the mark of their former glories. The *Football Echo* wrote of this harsh treatment: 'The attitude of some of the spectators at Ninian Park is to be deplored. They, to my mind, are very poor sports. They shout at one player, blame another, and harp that "but for the action of so-and-so it would have been a goal."'

If the fans could not blame the players for another loss then they turned on the opposition and the referee, as Stoke players and a match official found to their cost:

> In losing to Stoke this afternoon the City undoubtedly gave their worst display of the season. The game culminated with a most unfortunate demonstration against the referee and some of the visiting players. A kick was aimed at the referee, and an attempt was made to punch one of the visiting players.
>
> A section of the crowd acted like proper hooligans, and not content with their demonstration against the referee and the Stoke players, they made a couple of attempts to burst through the players' entrance seemingly with the idea of again getting at the referee.

With the team playing poorly, and the directors refusing to invest in new blood, many fans stayed away from Ninian Park. The *Football Express* said of this:

> Having enjoyed for something like six seasons the luxury of First Division football, followers of Cardiff City evidently do not relish the idea of having to be content with any other variety. This is apparent from the remarkable drop in gate receipts for the first two home matches compared with the corresponding games last season.
>
> I have it on reliable authority that the gates for the Preston and Hull City matches realised approximately £500 less than was taken in the games with Burnley and West Ham last September.

While 30,000 fans did attend Ninian Park for Cardiff's first-ever League encounter with rivals Swansea Town, it would prove to be the highest gate of the season as at times attendances dropped to as low as 8,000. This drop in attendances meant that Cardiff's finances suffered, and as a result the club was forced to accept a substantial offer from Manchester United for George McLachlan. They also accepted the much-needed sum of £8,000 from Middlesbrough for trio Joe Hillier, Jack Jennings and Freddie Warren. Stewart would be handed just £800 out of these proceeds to spend on Ralph Williams from Colwyn Bay.

The signing of Williams was, however, an inspired one, as shortly after he joined the club Cardiff enjoyed their best form of the season as he scored eight goals in seven games. For the first time that season Cardiff also won four successive League games, beating Blackpool, Bradford Park Avenue, Spurs and Millwall in the process.

The disappointing season ended on a high note as Cardiff beat Bury 5–1 at home, with Williams helping himself to a hat-trick. Since he had signed Williams had scored an impressive 11 goals in just 16 games. Yet the team's inconsistent form meant that they finished the season in eighth place and never threatened to gain promotion.

In the FA Cup the Bluebirds started the competition well when they shocked First Division Liverpool by beating them 2–1 at Anfield. Cardiff succumbed to defeat in the next round though as they lost to Sunderland.

In the Welsh Cup Cardiff met Rhyl in the Final as the two teams played out a goalless draw. The replay would not be played until October 1930 when Cardiff won the game 4–2, with Len Davies grabbing a hat-trick. This would turn out to be the last piece of silverware that Fred won in his glorious career.

Despite the fact that Fred was by now approaching 36 years of age, he could still occasionally roll back the years. In 1930, during an international game for Wales against Scotland at Hampden Park, Fred delivered what many would say was his career-defining performance in a game that would forever be branded 'Keenor and the Unknowns'.

As the game was to be played on a Saturday, when the English League had a full League program, teams were reluctant to release their Welsh internationals. Therefore, for the Scotland game, Ted Robbins, the Welsh manager, had no choice but to pick players from either Welsh League sides or from the non-Leagues to represent Wales. Fred was the only Football League player available and selected to play in the team that day.

The omens were not looking good for Wales as the last time they had resorted to fielding such a weak team they had been thrashed 7–0 by Ireland. Fred claimed that this was the worst game that he had ever played. Irish forward Joe Bambrick scored six of the goals that day and Fred felt responsible for a number of them: 'It must be unique for a player to score six goals in an international match but Joe will not mind me saying that I was "easy mate" that day. Everything I attempted went wrong, and the only time I got near the ball was near the end.'

The Scotland side was a far superior one to the Irish team and therefore it looked to all and sundry as being something of a suicide mission for the Welsh. On the day of the game the press predicted that it would be 'the slaughter of the innocents'.

Despite having a severely weakened team, Fred was determined that his beloved Wales would not be disgraced. He was never better than when he was an underdog; after all, despite being only 5ft 7in tall, and supposedly being a player of limited ability, he had become one of the great defenders in the game. In a subsequent interview Fred revealed how he had motivated the 'unknowns' before the clash with the Scots:

'I made a special request to Mr Ted Robbins to have the lads all to myself at least four hours before the match. This was readily granted. We had a quiet talk, then lunch, followed by some music from a borrowed gramophone. This brought us to within an hour and a half of the kick-off, but I had done what I could to create the right sort of team spirit. I did not want the youngsters to be thinking of Hampden Park with its atmosphere and intimidating Scottish roar. But now we had to talk about the game. For half an hour we had a heart-to-heart talk on tactics. I impressed upon the boys of the value of going for the ball quickly. I worked it out that if we could speed up our football the clever Scottish players would be put off their stride. We must be prepared to play hard, fast moving football from start to finish. It was going to be a real test in stamina and physical fitness. How those lads played! The names of every one of them figure in my book of heroes.'

Fred ended his talk with the time-honoured oath of the underdog: 'There's 11 of them, and 11 of us, and there's only one ball and it's ours.'

Unbelievably, after just six minutes, Wales went into the lead courtesy of Tommy Bamford. Despite defending for their lives Wales did eventually concede the equalising goal, but towards the end of the game it was the Welsh who looked most likely to grab the winner when Fred hit the crossbar with a fierce drive. The game eventually finished 1–1 and caused uproar when news of the result spread throughout the country. At the end of the game Ted Robbins was said to have wept unashamedly.

Fred had captained Wales that day like a man possessed. He had urged his players on by pleading and cursing, setting an example with his tireless running, and had put his ageing body on the line by delivering countless blocks and last-ditch tackles. Fred later revealed that he felt guilty about some of his cursing during the game: 'The boys were so keen that they did not want much rallying, but I was so completely captured by the cause that I am afraid I was rather severe upon some of them. It was just my way, and the rest of the players must have known this, because their response was amazing.'

Fred's cursing towards his own players was also noted by the referee, who warned him about his language. His retaliation was to let loose an even more colourful tirade on the referee himself. The referee said that his immediate reaction was to send Fred off the field, but he added: 'It suddenly came to me in a flash. Keenor was so engrossed in the game and getting everything out of his players that he did not know what he was saying. I did not send him off, and to this day I consider this was the best decision I ever made during my time as a referee.'

The *Scottish Daily Record and Mail* said of Fred's performance: 'Keenor was worth two men. Bandaged and limping at the last, he was the hero of the match. The pluckiest display in the history of international football.'

Fred recalled that the referee had told him that he had never experienced such an amazing display of courage on a football pitch and that many people who saw the game claimed that it was the best that he had ever played. Congratulatory messages poured in from every direction, including one from Canada.

After the game Fred was presented with an Airedale dog, which was 'the most popular member of the party on the happy journey home'. Sadly Fred lost the dog just a few days later when he opened his front door and it ran out, never to be seen again.

Such was the outstanding display from the 'Unknowns' that the Welsh public demanded that every one of the team be selected for the next international against England. Unfortunately, Fred could not lead the 'Unknowns' to victory in that game as they lost 4–0, but every single one of the players had deserved their place in the team following their heroics against Scotland.

Season 1930–31

The 1930 –31 season would prove to be Fred's last at Cardiff City. The team needed major surgery performed on it, but once more the club did not have any money to spare, and thus the directors were eager to offload the team's high earners.

Fred was still on his First Division salary and many at the club felt that his best days were behind him. The directors were reluctant to sell the fans' idol, however, for fear of the criticism they would receive. They therefore tried to force Fred to leave by offering him a financially reduced contract. Bartley Wilson approached Fred with the offer and told him: 'Fred. I'm sorry but I'm going to surprise you. We can only pay you £6 in the winter and £4 in the summer.'

This represented a significant pay cut, as at the time Fred was earning £8 a week during the season and £6 a week over the summer months. Yet Fred was not ready to be pushed out of Cardiff City and he surprisingly told Bartley Wilson: 'Bart. I'm going to surprise you too. I'm going to take it.'

Both Fred and Cardiff City had had an addition that summer with Fred celebrating the birth of his sixth child, Heather, and Fred Stewart signing George Emmerson from Middlesbrough. The Cardiff team was in desperate need of new blood but the club simply could not afford it. In a move designed to help get the most out of the threadbare squad, Billy Hardy, who had served the club as one of its most outstanding players for the previous 20 years, was appointed player-coach.

Desperate for one last hurrah in the blue shirt of Cardiff, Fred was actually feeling confident in the strength of the squad at the start of the season: 'We have a wealth of exceptionally good talent which with careful coaching and a smattering of experience will prove the basis of a brilliant side ere long. I have been honoured with the captaincy of the club this season. No captain in the English League has a better lot of boys than I have, and we are going to have a great season.'

Fred's judgement was terribly misplaced, as Cardiff endured a torrid start to the season, losing their first five games, including an opening-day defeat at rivals Swansea Town, a 3–0 defeat to Bury and a 6–3 home defeat to West Brom.

It was not until the eighth game of the season that Cardiff managed to finally win their first game of the campaign when they beat Plymouth Argyle 4–1. Not only was the squad a small one, but it was also suffering from an injury crisis, with no fewer than eight players on the sidelines, including Len Davies who was out with appendicitis.

Matters were not helped by the fact that Fred's playing abilities were also on the wane. He was by now fighting a losing battle against the tides of time and was also getting blamed for the deficiencies of his teammates: 'Keenor, also, I think, is deserving of criticism. He played a tremendously hard game and did his utmost to rouse the side, but when he realised that his defence was incapable of holding Cookson, why he did not make it his business to do so passes comprehension.'

With the team playing poorly drastic action was taken which resulted in Fred being dropped from the side, a decision backed by the local press: 'I do not agree with those who consider that Keenor has been a weak link in the team, neither do I support a chop-and-change policy as adopted in the case at Helsby. But the side as a whole has been so dreadfully unimpressive that it is worth while taking almost any step in an endeavour to impart a little ginger and team spirit qualities that have not existed to the slightest degree this season.'

However, the team performed like a rudderless ship without Fred in it and he was swiftly brought back into the fold. Again it was obvious to all that his ageing limbs were trying to do the work of his less able teammates. After a loss to Bristol City the *Football Echo* said: 'The truth is that Keenor is taking too much out of himself in trying to make good the deficiencies of his colleagues.'

On 1 November 1930, Fred scored his last goal for Cardiff City as the team beat Southampton 1–0. Cardiff's form looked like it was picking up after this result as they went on to beat Reading 5–0.

However, much of Cardiff's success had always been based around its sound defence, but advancing years and injuries meant that the once formidable rearguard was shipping goals at an alarming rate. In three successive away games they lost 4–1 at Wolves, 7–0 at Preston and 5–1 at Plymouth.

With so many goals being conceded the critics again looked towards Fred and asked whether he was worth his place in the team. The *Football Echo* defended Fred and stated that there was no one to replace him in any event: 'Keenor has got to show us that he is getting past it before anyone could think of leaving him out of the team. But supposed the worst happened, is there anyone to take Keenor's place? There is no one capable of emulating his amazing enthusiasm and industry.'

The directors of Cardiff City, however, felt that it was time for a change and therefore purchased John Galbraith from Clapton Orient, who was to be Fred's replacement. In a desperate last-ditch attempt to stay up they also allowed Fred Stewart to go out and sign Jim McCambridge from Everton and Albert Keating from Blackburn Rovers. The team was sinking without a trace, however, and the new additions failed to improve results.

The signing of Galbraith had meant Fred's days at the club appeared numbered. The *Football Echo* felt this was a harsh way to treat a player of Fred's stature:

'There never was a pivot who infused greater energy and industry into his play than Keenor has during his wonderful career, and I am rather afraid that Galbraith, or whoever else may become Keenor's successor, will be judged by the Keenor standard rather than by that of the average pivot, who is more orthodox and often less conspicuous than Keenor might be, although rendering his side equally good service.

'The position of Keenor has become rather complicated by the arrival of Galbraith, and, while the ex-Clapton Orient man must be given his chance, it seems very rough luck on such a grand old warrior and fighter as Keenor that he should now be struggling for a place in the team.'

Indeed, the defence did not improve with Galbraith in the side and he was said to have had an 'unhappy' debut in a loss to Bristol City. Despite losing his place in the team to Galbraith and at times to local lad Eddie Jenkins, Fred felt no bitterness towards them. In fact, as Jenkins recalls, Fred did all he could to help them: 'I was versatile. I played in five different positions while with Cardiff – right and left-back and the three half-back positions. Fred Keenor was on his way out and I was his possible replacement, but it was very difficult to follow such a great player. He took me under his wing and showed me the ropes and, in fact, I played six games with Fred. I remember he told me I'd done well in my first match at Bradford – but next time I shouldn't hang too far back. He gave me some useful tips about marking. Fred could be a bit crude and extremely forthright but what a player. He never gave less than 100 per cent. If it was possible he would have tried even harder than that.'

On 17 January 1931, Cardiff beat Port Vale 2–1 but would then win only one more game that season. The team would score just eight goals during those 17 winless games and as a result they would be relegated before the season had ended.

The supporters, who had grown up with Cardiff being one of the leading teams in the country, became disillusioned at the state of the club and subsequently started to desert the team in droves. For the final home game of the season against Bury, only 5,000 fans showed up, the club's lowest League attendance since 1910. Cardiff City, for the first time in their history, would play the 1931–32 season in Division Three South of the Football League.

In an interview, Fred outlined the many reasons why he felt Cardiff had managed to get relegated:

1. As a team we were not playing well.
2. We missed that little bit of luck which we had in previous seasons.

3. Key players were transferred. This disturbed the smooth working of the side.

4. Having been lulled into a false sense of security by their run of success, the club's efforts to strengthen the side were made too late.

The team fared little better in the Cup competitions during this disastrous season when they were firstly knocked out of the FA Cup in the first round by Brentford and then crashed out of the Welsh Cup at the semi-final stage to Shrewsbury Town.

On 6 April 1931, Fred's 19-year association with Cardiff City came to an end when he played his last game for the club. It was fitting that the game would be against Fred's old adversaries Spurs, with whom he had enjoyed some titanic tussles with throughout his career.

The Spurs game was also to be the final game in Len Davies's Cardiff career. Len had been with the club since 1919, and despite missing the all-important penalty against Birmingham in 1924, he had scored 184 goals in 369 games. He is still incredibly the only player to have scored over 100 League goals for the Bluebirds.

Davies did not sign off with a goal against the Lilywhites, but Fred did get a clean sheet as the game finished scoreless. The clean sheet had helped Fred deliver a reminder to his critics, and the directors of the club, that he could still play at this level: 'The outstanding players against Spurs – the men who really kept the side together – were the "veterans": Hardy, who played as well as ever; and Keenor, still a marvellous bundle of energy and the club's best centre-half in spite of what the directors may think.'

On previous occasions Fred's threats to leave Cardiff had fallen through, but this time around both Fred, and the club, knew that the time had come to finally part ways. As a result, at the end of the season, Fred was released from the club he had loved and served so valiantly.

As the season had gone on Fred had become increasingly frustrated with the drop in standards at his beloved club. Gone was the calibre of players such as Jimmy Gill and Hughie Ferguson, and Fred had for once found it difficult to motivate himself, and his lesser-skilled teammates, to play to the level that his high standards demanded. It is rumoured that during his last few months at the club, such was Fred's inability to accept just how far Cardiff's fortunes had fallen, that he had argued with Fred Stewart, the directors and fellow players, by delivering a withering assessment of their performances. His departure from Cardiff City was not too dissimilar from the way in which Roy Keane left Manchester United: both men were proud, fearless winners unable to come to terms with suddenly becoming also-rans.

In his time at Cardiff City Fred had immortalised himself, not only by racking up 505 first-team appearances, but also by being a vitally important part of the team that had seen the club rise from the ranks of the Southern League to become one of the best teams in the Football League. He had come within a whisker of becoming a First Division champion and had, of course, captained the side to victory in the 1927 Cup Final. In *The Who's Who of Cardiff City Players*, Fred is described as 'quite simply the greatest Bluebird of all'.

CHAPTER 8

THE POST-CARDIFF CITY YEARS

Life after Cardiff City

At the age of 37 many expected Fred to retire, but he was not yet ready to quit the game he loved. So in the summer of 1931, Fred and his family made a surprise move and relocated to Crewe, where Fred spent the next four years of his career making a total of 123 appearances for Third Division North team Crewe Alexandra.

At Crewe, a club that had never played in a higher League than the Third Division, Fred was viewed as a big fish in a small pond; such was his high standing in the game as an FA Cup-winner and captain of Wales. He was by far the most high-profile player to have ever played for the club and as a result his presence in the team guaranteed a bigger attendance at Gresty Road; indeed, when Fred was injured, and unable to play, Crewe would not announce the news for fear that it would affect the gate.

In his first season at the club, Fred seemed to benefit from a change of scenery, as he rolled back the years to lead the team to sixth place in the Third Division. This was the highest position that Crewe had finished in for 10 years. Fred was frustrated that the team did not go on to achieve promotion that season as he felt that there was a 'nucleus of a very good side'; however, the club's limited finances meant that it could not afford to add the one or two players that the team needed in order to get out of the Division.

In that first year at Crewe, Fred also played in two remarkable games against League leaders Lincoln City. Crewe won the first game 8–0, but then lost 5–0 in the away game. There were extenuating circumstances in the away game defeat, however, as Fred was knocked unconscious for an hour after he stuck his head in the way of a shot on goal. While he was off the field Lincoln scored all five of their goals. The footballs used during this period were, of course, made of thick leather, and on a wet day the ball would soak up the water and become progressively heavier. If you were unfortunate enough to get struck on the head by such a ball it was the equivalent of someone hitting you with a dumbbell.

Another memorable game from Fred's time in the North West occurred when Crewe played their local rivals Stockport County. Fred was never the most popular player for opposing fans, due to frequently upsetting them with his uncompromising tackles, and this game was no different. At the end of the match, as Fred left the field, a Stockport supporter ran onto the pitch and hit Fred across the shoulders with a walking stick. Fred turned round to defend himself but his teammates dragged him away as more spectators ran to confront him.

When Fred had returned to the relative safety of the dressing room he thought that the incident was over. However, as Fred recalls, one of the enraged fans managed to get inside the dressing room and confronted him: 'A section of the crowd continued to demonstrate outside, and in the confusion one chap who must have had more determination than common sense got into our dressing room. "Where's Keenor?" he shouted. "Ah there he is". He rushed over and adopted a fighting attitude, but my colleagues intervened and he was bundled outside. That properly put the fat in the fire. I was escorted to the railway station by a number of policemen followed by a large crowd.'

While Fred played for Crewe, Muriel Keenor gave birth to their seventh and last child, Graham. Graham would eventually go on to become club secretary of Cardiff City, much to the delight of his father.

Fred might have felt that now he was playing for Crewe, in the Third Division, that his international days were behind him; however, he was shocked, and pleasantly surprised, when he was called-up to play for Wales against Scotland at Hampden Park.

That day the Welsh team hammered the Scots 5–2. It was the first time that Wales had beaten Scotland at Hampden Park since 1906 and the game was therefore a fitting end to Fred's fantastic international career.

Fred claims that in his last-ever international he did 'more running about in that match than any other' as he was faced with the task of keeping the famous Scotland and Arsenal player, Alex James, quiet.

Fred would later claim that in all his years as a professional it was Alex James who was the best player that he had faced: 'In my opinion easily the greatest footballer of the last decade. There is not a "trick in the trade" he does not know. It's going to take Arsenal all their time and a lot of money to replace this wee Scot. He knew every move, and seemed to think that move ahead of every player.'

With his international days now behind him Fred said of representing his country: 'I shall always be proud of the small part I was able to play in bringing honour to Wales. *Cymru am byth!*'

At the age of 41 Fred's career as a professional footballer had finally come to an end. He still could not quite bring himself to cut his ties completely with the game, however, so he signed for semi-professional team Oswestry Town, where he played one season as player-manager before succumbing to ill-health.

Fred was suffering, not only due to the physical commitments of having played professional football for 23 years, but also because he was a heavy smoker and drinker, coupled with being diagnosed as a diabetic, a condition which was harder to treat back then than it is now. Fred had given all he had to the game and he was now left battered, ill and penniless.

With Fred out of football, and unable to find any other work due to his ill-health, he struggled to support his wife and seven children. His circumstances became increasingly difficult, as he was also not able to claim the dole.

When the news of what had become of Fred was heard in South Wales it was greeted with shock and disbelief that their former warrior had fallen on such hard times. Such was the esteem that Fred commended in his native country that the Football Association of Wales not only forwarded Fred some money, but it also ran a fund for him. Furthermore, admirers sent cheques to newspaper offices in order for the money to be sent on to Fred. In a sign of the regard that the fans of Cardiff City still had for their hero, a blanket was also carried around Ninian Park during a match by former players and local theatre stars, so people could throw in their donations.

While Fred was confined to his hospital bed, receiving treatment for his diabetes, he still followed the results of his much-loved Cardiff City and said 'I get a real thrill when I hear that the City have won.'

It seems that the downturn in Fred's life had also coincided with a downturn in Cardiff City's fortunes. Since Fred had left Ninian Park the club had unbelievably finished in the relegation zone of the Third Division South and had to humiliatingly apply for re-election to the Football League.

The club's poor fortunes meant that the press transformed Fred into the figurehead of a golden era that had long since passed away. The local press even printed cartoons of the shadow of Fred, a representation of former glories, looming large over Ninian Park and the current team.

Fred was still very much the Cardiff hero and as a result he was invited by the *Football Echo* to write a series of articles giving his view on the 'modern' game. Not only did this give Fred the opportunity to talk about the game he loved, but it also provided him with some much-needed income. The articles that he wrote in 1937 reveal just how little the usual debates surrounding the game have changed in the intervening years.

For instance, in one article Fred felt that the very best players in the game deserved to be paid more money. Of course, unlike today's well-rewarded professional players, this was during the era when even a top player did not earn much more than the average man. Fred wrote:

The most a player can earn is £8 in the winter and £6 in the summer. In making a plea for higher wages I do not mean to infer that all players, even some of those in the First Division, are worth this, but surely the stars are entitled to more money.

After all, the tip-top player receives more attention from the public and the opposition and he has to put much more into the game. How many times when tactics are being discussed have we concentrated on the 'star' footballer. 'Stop him and we stand a chance' is a common phrase at these pow-wows. This does not necessarily mean that shady tricks are going to be used to achieve this end, but the 'star' is the most marked man in football.

Then, again, many people attend matches only to see the 'star'. This might be unfair to the other performers but it is a fact.

In another article Fred bemoaned the use of illegal inducements in the game, which of course we are very familiar with today due to the word *'bung'* constantly being seen in the sports pages:

I know for a fact that some players on being transferred have received more money 'under the table' than 'on top of it', but only one or two have publicly exposed the evil.

Here are two experiences of mine. One club offered me the management of a fully-licensed hotel on a three-year guarantee as part of my transfer, while another offered to give me a business worth at least £200. I tell you frankly that these offers were seriously considered by me, but I came to the conclusion that the risk involved was too great. Furthermore, I loved the game so much that the very thought of being found out sent cold shivers down my spine.

Recently we have seen calls for the game to introduce more referees on the field; indeed, in the Europa League we have seen a trial where further officials have been placed behind the goals. In fact, as far back as 1937 this was being debated, although Fred was 'against the suggestion that two referees would be the remedy'.

With the outpouring of love and donations from the people of Cardiff, Fred managed to get back on his feet. After leaving hospital he decided to relocate to Lamberhurst, a small village outside Tunbridge Wells, in order to enjoy the fresh air and nurse himself back to health.

While he lived in the area Fred helped Muriel run a corner shop and also set up a small poultry business in which he would buy young chicks, fatten them up and then sell them at Christmas. In later years he would also find work in a petrol refinery in nearby Hove. This was all a far cry from his glory years as one of the top footballers in the country, yet he never complained.

Such was Fred's resolve and dedication to work that even after he fell from a loft, breaking a few ribs in the process, he shrugged off his injuries and was back in work within a few days. Fred's son-in-law, Brian Jones, also says that he would frequently see Fred walking the five miles to Tunbridge Wells from his Lamberhurst home in order to remain fit.

Shortly after arriving in the small Kent town word had spread that there was a football legend among them. As a result Fred was invited to become player-manager of Tunbridge Wells Rangers. Though Fred was still unwell he was unable to resist a return to the game in some capacity.

Fred's son, Graham, recalls his father's time at Tunbridge Wells:

> My first recollections were of Dad actually playing for Tunbridge Wells Rangers. He did everything there – including tending to the pitch!
>
> I remember him once coming off the field and going into the dressing room with quite a stud mark on the front of his shin. He went to a little box where he kept a bottle of iodine, and that made an impression on me – Dad was pretty hard! He was still a good footballer but his age meant that he couldn't do as much work on the park as he wanted.

As well as coaching Tunbridge Wells Rangers, Fred also managed the Lamberhurst junior football side, for which his young sons played. It seems that his sons inherited Fred's talent for football as the Lamberhurst side won numerous trophies under Fred's stewardship.

Though Fred was regarded as a football legend in the area he was always reluctant to brag. Brian Jones recalls that he would never raise the subject of his achievements himself, but if pressed on the subject he would eventually discuss them. Fred would, however, always insist that at Cardiff City he had been lucky to play in such a fantastic team, under such a great manager, and without their help he would not have achieved as much as he eventually did in the game.

In later years Brian Jones would marry Fred's daughter, Heather (who had inherited her mother's musical talent), and the two of them performed together in a dance band for many years. When the band played in the local village Fred and Muriel would enjoy going to watch them.

With the fresh air of Kent helping Fred return to health he decided to volunteer for the Territorial Army. His application reveals that he was a 'man of good character' and he was subsequently admitted to the 314th Kent Regiment of the Royal Engineers, in which he served as a Sapper.

However, on 18 June 1939 Fred was discharged from serving in the TAs due to his ongoing problems with diabetes. This may have been a blessing in disguise, as on 1 September 1939 World War Two broke out following the German invasion of Poland.

Due to his ill-health Fred had no option but to remain in Tunbridge Wells, while his two sons, Frederick and Alfred, enlisted in order to fight for their country. To the intense dismay of Muriel and Fred both sons were tragically killed during the war.

Alfred Keenor, the boy who had once been a promising goalkeeper, had died a heroic death mirroring his father's sense of duty and courage. He had been flying a plane over the French village of Fruges when he was shot down. The plane started to fall from the sky and was set to crash into the village, where it would have killed many of its inhabitants. Alfred was obviously aware of this as he somehow managed to steer the plane away from Fruges and crash-land in a nearby field. Unfortunately, he did not survive the crash.

In later years, Fred's daughter Heather and her husband Brian took Muriel to visit Alfred's grave in France. Upon arriving in the village it was clear that the people of Fruges had not forgotten Alfred's heroic deed and Muriel was afforded a hero's welcome.

With the war ending in August 1945 Fred and his family continued to live in Kent. Yet as time wore on Fred became restless and yearned for a return to his home town. He eventually returned to Cardiff in 1958 and he became a store man with Cardiff Corporation's Building Department.

Sadly, in 1967 Muriel Keenor died in tragic circumstances, which almost claimed the life of Fred as well. A gas leak originating from outside their Grangetown home had resulted in their house being filled with poisonous gas. Consequently Muriel Keenor was poisoned in the front room of the house and died while Fred only just managed to survive after being found unconscious.

The tragedy could have been much worse, however, as every morning Fred would religiously pack a pipe full of tobacco and light it up. For some reason, on the day of the gas leak, he failed to follow this routine and it saved his life, as if he had done so the house would have exploded the moment he had lit his pipe.

After being found unconscious by a neighbour, Fred was hospitalised. The fumes had left him seriously ill and it looked doubtful that he would survive. Brian Jones recalls that Fred's son Graham would frequently ring his wife, Heather, and inform them that they needed to urgently drive to Cardiff, from their Lamberhurst home, as it looked as if Fred would not make it through the day.

However, Brian recalls that upon arriving at the hospital Fred would have somehow made a miraculous recovery and he would be sat up in bed joking with the nurses and his fellow patients. Even in ill-health he was the focal point of his ward, and he would entertain fellow patients with comments to the hospital porter such as: 'Call yourself a porter? I've been waiting days for a train to arrive to get me out of here!'

Fred did eventually recover but he was heartbroken at the loss of his beloved wife and still suffering from the after-effects of the gas leak. It was decided that he required full-time care and he was admitted to a nursing home in the Cardiff district of Gabalfa. During this time devoted fans of Cardiff City, including my father, would pick Fred up from his nursing home and take the old stalwart to watch his beloved Bluebirds play at Ninian Park.

My father recalled that as they entered the Grand Stand the crowd rose as one to applaud the returning warrior. Though Fred was now a pensioner this did not diminish his enthusiasm for the game as he cheered as loudly as any fan and bemoaned those players whom he did not think were putting in the required effort.

On 19 October 1972, at the age of 78, the old Cardiff City and Wales hero passed away. He was subsequently buried in Cardiff's Thornhill Crematorium.

Trevor Morris, the Welsh FA Secretary, said on the day of Fred's death:

> Fred Keenor will go down in history as one of the greatest players and greatest character ever produced by Wales.

Ernie Curtis, Fred's teammate from 1927, recalled Fred's never-say-die attitude:

> Fred Keenor never gave up. He had such a fighting spirit that, to me, he was one of the biggest-hearted players of all time.

It is only fitting that Fred himself should have the final words on his life, as he wrote as far back as 1937:

> It has been a personal pleasure to ponder on the 'good old days' because the best part of my life was spent at Cardiff. Football is one of the greatest sporting games I know, and I am proud of the part I played in it. Looking back it has been a full and active life. I have had it all – thrills, excitement, success, the laughter and – yes, the tears.
>
> That is the end boys. If you have derived as much pleasure from reading these reminiscences as I have in writing them, then the benefits have been mutual. UP THE CITY!

CHAPTER 9

FRED'S LEGACY

The Spirit of Fred Keenor Lives On

Fred Keenor may have died over 37 years ago, but the fight to remember his legacy still lives on. While Fred is always referred to 'as the greatest of the Bluebirds' there has never been a permanent tribute erected to honour either him or the 1927 Cup-winning team. This is despite the fact that there are numerous other statues of Welsh sports stars in South Wales.

However, in 2007 a Cardiff City fan by the name of Mike Inker started a petition in order to get a statue of Fred erected in Cardiff. Mike stated: 'Fred Keenor and the 1927 team haven't had the recognition their efforts justify and we're determined to put that right. There remains a lot of work to do, including raising the necessary funds, but with City fans and the people of Cardiff and Wales behind us, we are very confident of raising the funds required.'

On 17 December 2009, as I was coming to the end of writing this book, it was announced that sculptor Roger Andrews had been appointed to sculpt the statue of Fred. Andrews said: 'It is an honour and privilege to be appointed as the sculptor for the Fred Keenor statue. I am sure the statue will be seen as iconic by fans of Cardiff City Football Club and an outstanding memorial to Fred and the 1927 FA Cup-winning team.'

All that remains before the statue can be created is to raise the sum of £75,000. Fred's nephew, Graham, said of the prospect of raising the necessary funds: 'I'm confident fans, businesses and people across South Wales will get behind this hugely worthwhile fundraiser.'

Cardiff City chairman Peter Ridsdale and the Cardiff City Supporters Trust have promised to back Graham's appeal for the funding and do all that they can to assist him.

The statue's location has not yet been finalised, but it is thought that it will be placed outside Cardiff City's new stadium so that the spirit of Fred will hopefully be able to inspire the current crop of players at the club.

As mentioned in the introduction to this book, in 2008 Fred became a hot topic of conversation when Cardiff City amazingly shocked the football world when, for the first time since 1927, they reached the FA Cup Final. While Cardiff could not repeat the success of the famous 1927 team, many nostalgic tales were told in the local press and on the national news about Fred's achievements in the blue shirt of Cardiff City. The coverage meant a new legion of football fans were made aware of Fred's heroics.

In November 2009, Brian Jones saved up the money in order to replace Fred's weather-beaten gravestone at Thornhill Crematorium. The new black granite gravestone marking Fred's final resting place was inscribed with the following words:

Cherished Memories of FREDERICK CHARLES KEENOR
Capt. CARDIFF CITY – WALES
DIED OCT. 19TH 1972 AGED 78 YEARS
Also in Remembrance of his Beloved Wife MURIEL

Now that Fred is set to have a statue erected of him, has a new gravestone and has finally had a book written about his life, it seems that he is getting the recognition that he has long deserved.

Fred may be gone, but he is most certainly not forgotten. His family and fans are determined that his legacy will be remembered forever so that future generations will know not only Fred Keenor, the FA Cup-winner, but also Fred Keenor the war veteran, captain colossus, leader of men, a credit to the game of football and a Welsh hero.